Shore Fishes
of Hawai'i

John E. Randall

UNIVERSITY OF HAWAI'I PRESS
Honolulu

© 1996 John E. Randall

First published by Natural World Press, Vida, Oregon, 1996
Reprinted by University of Hawai'i Press, 1998, 1999

Printed in the United States of America

09 08 07 06 05 04   9 8 7 6 5 4

Library of Congress Cataloging-in-Publication Data

Randall, John E., 1924–
   Shore fishes of Hawaii / John E. Randall
      p.   cm.
   Includes index.
   ISBN 0-8248-2182-3 (pbk.)
   1. Marine fishes—Hawaii—Identification. 2. Marine
   fishes—Hawaii—Pictorial works. I. Title.
   QL636.5.H3R359 1996
   597.09969—dc20   96-30157
                                                             CIP

Printed by Worzalla

ACKNOWLEDGMENTS

Many persons have helped the author in the preparation or production of this book. Foremost is my wife Helen who assisted in innumerable ways, including review of the manuscript. Bruce C. Mundy also deserves special mention for his critical review of the manuscript. Thanks are due to the following persons for assistance in diving, in collecting fishes, or curating fish specimens: Gerald R. Allen, Paul M. Allen, Paul Anka, Marjorie Awai, Ken and Linda Bail, Richard E. Brock, Lori Buckley, Bruce A. Carlson, Kent E. Carpenter, Lisa Choquette and Tom Shockley, E.H. Chave, Thomas A. Clarke, Ron and Barbara Crabtree, Jane B. Culp, Norman M. Estin, John Farrington, David and Jennifer Fleetham, Dennis Fontany, Ofer Gon, David W. Greenfield, Hamilton and Nancy Harris, Alan Hong, Therese Hayes, Philip Helfrich, Ronald R. Holcom, John P. Hoover, Steve Kaiser, Hiroshi Kato, Tomo Kimura, Phillip S. Lobel, Rhett M. McNair, Mark S. Mohlmann, Theresa A. Moore, Anthony Nahacky, David S. Norquist, Loreen R. O'Hara, Henry Y. Okamoto, Bob and Tina Owens, James D. Parrish, Sarah Peck, Luciano Perino, Roger A. Pfeffer, Corydon Pittman, Lisa A. Privitera, Richard L. Pyle, Ed and Sue Robinson, Jim and Julie Robinson, Nelson Santos, Mike Severns and Pauline Fiene, Keoki Stender, Lewis and Dara Strauss, Arnold Y. Suzumoto, Guy Tamashiro, Walter H. Tamashiro, A. Bradley Tarr, Leighton R. Taylor, Spencer W. Tinker, Gordon W. Tribble, Robin S. Waples, Paul N. Warren, Lester Zukeran, and especially John L. Earle. And finally, for encouragement and support, Roland S. Boreham, Jr.; for excellence in publication, Russell and Blyth Carpenter.

TABLE OF CONTENTS

ALPHABETICAL LIST OF SPECIES AND
FISH WATCHING RECORD

(Check the box when you've seen a fish, put the date and/or location on the line.)

INTRODUCTION

The primary purpose of this book is to provide for the identification of the fishes that snorkelers or SCUBA divers are most apt to encounter on reefs or adjacent habitats. A total of 340 species are included. Because many of the species have juveniles of different form and color, and some, such as most of the wrasses and parrotfishes, have different sexual color patterns, it is necessary to have two or three illustrations for these species. In order to cover so many species in a book of this size, the species accounts are short. However, the most important characteristics to identify a fish are provided. In addition, the size attained by the species (given as total length in inches or feet, with the metric equivalent) and its distribution are given. If a Hawaiian fish is wide-ranging in the warm seas of the Indian Ocean and the central and western Pacific, we say that it is Indo-Pacific in its distribution.

Each species account begins with the American common name (not everyone agrees on all the common names), followed by the Hawaiian name (when known), and the scientific name (in italics). The scientific name consists of two parts; the first is the genus (capitalized) and the second the species name. Some species of fish are so different that they are in a genus by themselves, but most genera (plural of genus) contain two or more species. The name of the person or persons who first described a new species of fish and provided its scientific name is given after the species name, followed by the year when the name was published. A person's name in parentheses means that he or she placed the fish in another genus than the one in current use.

The Hawaiians did not have names for many of the smaller fishes of no importance to them, or they applied only a general name (like **'o'opu** for gobies). Often the Hawaiian general name was followed by a secondary name (hence their fish names were equivalent to the genus and species of scientific names). Some of the secondary names have been lost. For example, it is likely that the ancient Hawaiians had secondary names for at least some of the different squirrelfishes and soldierfishes (Holocentridae), but all we know today is the general name **'ala'ihi** for all squirrelfishes, and **'ū'ū** for the soldierfishes.

When pronouncing Hawaiian words, it is well to remember that every vowel is sounded. The punctuation mark ' in a Hawaiian word denotes the glottal stop, a common feature of Polynesian languages. It indicates a brief pause at this point in the pronunciation of a word. At one time in the past there was a consonant where each glottal stop is now shown. The macron over a vowel, as in **'ū'ū**, indicates a longer sounding of the vowel than usual.

The reef and shore fishes of Hawai'i are classified in 99 different families. Family names end in "idae," hence the butterflyfish family is Chaetodontidae. A separate account is given for each of the families in order to provide in-formation that applies to the species, in general. If, for ex-ample, all species of a family feed on the animals of the plankton, this is mentioned only in the text for the family and not repeated for each species. After the fam-ily account, the fishes are ar-ranged alphabetically by genus and species. The presentation of the families is in phylogenetic order, i.e. the most primitive (the sharks and rays) first and what we believe to be the most highly evolved (the puffers and porcupinefishes) last.

Hawai'i represents a subprovince of the vast tropical and sub-tropical Indo-Pacific region which stretches from the Red Sea and coast of East Africa to the easternmost islands of Oceania (Hawai'i and Easter Island). In other words, the composition of the Hawaiian marine life is different enough from the rest of the Indo-Pacific to be treated as a distinct faunal subregion.

Many of the inshore fishes of Hawai'i are the same all the way to East Africa, but a surprising 24.3% are endemic to Hawai'i (i.e. found no where else in the world). This is the highest percentage of endemism for warm-water marine fishes. The inshore fish fauna of the Hawaiian Islands is distinctive not only in its numerous en-demic species but in the many groups of fishes that are lacking.

There are no skates (Rajidae), only five shallow-water rays, and no species of the following families of bony fishes that are well represented in continental and many insular seas of the rest of the Indo-Pacific: toadfishes (Batrachoididae), flatheads (Platycephalidae), dottybacks (Pseudochromidae), terapons (Teraponidae), fusiliers (Caesionidae), breams (Nemipteridae), porgies (Sparidae), drums and croakers (Sciaenidae), whitings (Sillaginidae), mojarras (Gerreidae), ponyfishes (Leiognathidae), sweepers (Pempheridae), rabbitfishes (Siganidae), jawfishes (Opistognathidae), and clingfishes (Gobiescocidae). Also there are only two native groupers (one additional species, the **roi** (*Cephalopholis argus*) has been introduced, no native snappers of the genus *Lutjanus* (three have been established by introductions), and only one emperor (Lethrinidae), the **mu** (*Monotaxis grandoculis*).

The explanation for Hawaii's unique fish fauna lies in its isolation, not only geographically, but hydrographically. Pelagic fishes such as the larger tunas, the billfishes, and some sharks are able to swim the great distance that separates the Hawaiian Islands from any other islands or continents in the Pacific, but shore fishes are dependent for their distribution on passive transport as larvae in ocean currents. As would be expected, the fish families that have a high percentage of species in the Hawaiian Islands compared to elsewhere tend to be those with species that have long larval life, such as the moray eels (Muraenidae) and surgeonfishes (Acanthuridae), whereas the families that contain mainly species with short larval life, such as the gobies (Gobiidae), blennies (Blenniidae), and cardinalfishes (Apogonidae), are not as well represented in Hawai'i as in the rest of the Indo-Pacific region.

The prevailing current in Hawai'i is the North Equatorial Current, but this is not a likely route for the colonization by shore fishes to the Hawaiian Islands. Any larvae of fishes coming to the Hawaiian area in this current system would originate in the cool sea of southern California or northern Mexico. Not only is the transport time too great for the 2300 mile (3800 km) journey for most larvae to survive, but nearly all would find the sea of Hawai'i too warm. Based on the present current system, most fish larvae would probably arrive at the Northwestern Hawaiian Islands via an eddy of the warm Kuroshio Current that bathes southern Japan and heads northeast. For a species to establish itself in the Hawaiian Islands, many larvae would have to settle out in the same area so that at least two, one of each sex, would reach maturity, and successfully reproduce.

Given the distance involved, the vagaries of spawning and eddy systems, and the perfect timing and spacing needed for all factors, it is obvious that a successful colonization of Hawai'i by a shore fish would not happen often. Only by realizing the geologic time scale can we understand how Hawai'i has so many reef and shore fishes. The Hawaiian Islands first emerged from the sea floor of the large tectonic plate known as the Pacific Plate from a volcanic hot spot in the earth's crust more than 70 million years ago. The newest island of the Hawaiian Chain, Hawai'i (still with an active volcano), is on this spot today, but like others before it, is being moved about 10 cm per year (4 inches) in a WNW direction toward northern Japan. The more distant from the hot spot, the more eroded are the islands; those of the Northwestern Hawaiian Islands, such as Midway and Kure that are over 1500 miles (2500 km) from the island of Hawai'i, are only low islands or atolls. Still farther we find the former high islands are now submerged seamounts. A chain of these, the Emperor Seamounts, lead toward the Kamchatka Peninsula, indicating more northerly movement of the Pacific Plate in the past.

Many of the fish which are found only in Hawai'i have what we call a sister species elsewhere in the Indo-Pacific region, and we can speculate with some degree of confidence that the Hawaiian species arose from this close relative or that the two had a common ancestor. Other Hawaiian endemic fishes, however, have no obvious close relatives, suggesting that they have been in the islands for a very long time and the progenitor stock has not survived or is so different now that it is not recognized. We call these relics. Examples are the Masked Angelfish (*Genicanthus personatus*) and the Bluestripe Butterflyfish (*Chaetodon fremblii*). The Redbarred Hawkfish (*Cirrhitops fasciatus*) has a very interesting disjunct distribution: Hawaiian Islands and Madagascar and Mauritius in the southwest Indian Ocean. This hawkfish must have been widely distributed in the Indo-Pacific region at one time, but is surviving now only as a relic at these isolated islands.

The endemic fishes of Hawai'i are often the most common members of their genera. Examples are the Saddle Wrasse (*Thalassoma duperrey*), the most abundant and ubiquitous reef fish in Hawai'i, and the Milletseed Butterflyfish (*Chaetodon miliaris*). One might surmise that their success as species is due to their having long resided in Hawaiian waters; therefore, they may have had more time to become fully adapted to the Hawaiian environment than later arrivals.

The Hawaiian Chain spans a range of latitude from 19°N to 28°N. Anyone diving in the northwest end of the archipelago will soon notice that the sea is much cooler there. As might be expected, there are fishes one can find in the main Hawaiian Islands (i.e. Kauai to Hawai'i) that are not seen in Midway or Kure, and conversely, there are species at the northwest end of the chain that do not occur in the main islands. Some fishes which inhabit only deep water in the main islands may be found in diving depths in the Northwestern Hawaiian Islands.

Johnston Island, lying about 750 miles (1250 km) southwest of the Hawaiian Islands, is an outlier of the Hawaiian marine biota. When the distribution of a fish is given as Hawaiian Islands, it usually includes Johnston Island.

It is necessary to use some scientific terminology when giving the principal diagnostic characteristics of families or species of fishes or listing what they eat. A Glossary of scientific terms is given at the back of the book before the Index. The diagram at the end of this chapter presents the most important external parts of a fish.

Most bony fishes have both spines and soft rays in their dorsal and anal fins. Spines are not branched, not finely segmented, generally not flexible, and usually sharp, whereas soft rays are segmented, flexible, and often branched. To differentiate these two kinds of fin rays, the count of the spines is given in Roman numerals and that of soft rays in Arabic. Thus a dorsal fin-ray count of X,12 would indicate ten spines and twelve soft rays. In describing the color markings on fishes, the term bar is used for a vertically oriented band and stripe for a horizontal (or lengthwise) one.

The fish photographs in this book were taken by the author, many in three of the marine parks of the State of Hawai'i: Hanauma Bay, O'ahu; Molokini off Maui; and Kealakekua Bay, Hawai'i (see illustrations). No fishing is allowed in these reserves. Because of the numerous divers and snorkelers that visit the sanctuaries, none of whom are spearing or netting, the fishes become accustomed to the presence of man in the sea, and most can be more closely approached than in areas that are not protected. Also their behavior is more normal, and one can watch them feeding, spawning, or interacting with other marine life.

Hawai'i is woefully lacking in enough Marine Life Conservation Districts (MLCD) for a maritime state that depends heavily on tourists, many of whom are divers or snorkelers. The few such reserves that are established are being too heavily visited by tourists and residents alike.

Creating more MLCDs would serve the purpose not only of providing more reserves where people can enjoy the marine life, but also taking some of the stress off the existing parks and insuring that more areas exist where fishes can grow to full reproductive maturity. Their larvae will then seed the other reef and shore areas in the islands that are currently being greatly overfished. When a female fish first becomes mature, she lays relatively few eggs in her first spawnings. If she grows to twice her length at maturity, her egg productivity does not merely double; it increases enormously because the enlargement of the ovary with growth is not linear but volumetric. Furthermore, some families of fishes such as groupers, hawkfishes, wrasses, and parrotfishes commence mature life as females; they are able to change sex later in life to males. What will happen to the reproduction if they are caught before they become males?

At least 10 percent of the coastline of the Hawaiian Islands should be set aside as reserves in which no fishing is allowed. The result will be far better fishing in the 90% of our coast where fishing is allowed.

Hanauma Bay, located on Oah'u 10 miles east of Waikiki, is the result of the sea breaking through the outer wall of a volcanic crater. The bay became a Marine Life Conservation District in 1967; it has had as many as two million visitors a year. More MLCDs are needed for the State of Hawai'i.

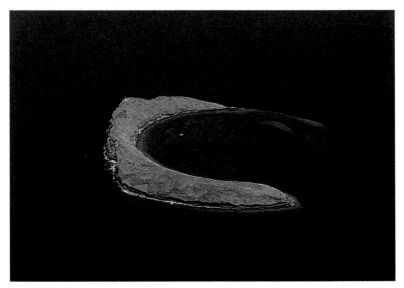

Crescentic Molokini off the southwest coast of Maui is the result of an undersea explosion. It became a Marine Life Conservation District in 1977. Every morning it is visited by many dive and snorkel vessels.

(Photograph by Robert J. Shallenberger.)

A trimaran has just discharged its cargo of snorkelers to admire the undersea life of fully protected Kealakekua Bay on the Kona Coast of Hawai'i. The structure to the upper right is Captain Cook's monument; the famous navigator was killed by Hawaiians not far from this site.

Kealakekua Bay became the third Marine Life Conservation District in the Hawaiian Islands in 1969. The Bay is protected from the open ocean swell and is calm most of the time. The color of its water changes from green, in the inshore areas, to a deep blue at a depth of about 100 feet.

External Parts of a Fish

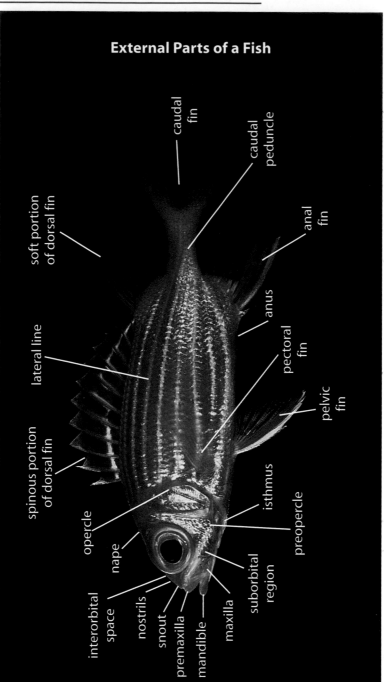

SHARKS AND RAYS (CHONDRICHTHYES)

SHARKS

Only about 360 species of sharks are known in the world, compared to approximately 24,000 bony fishes. In spite of their low number of species, sharks play a major role in the seas of the world. Many are the top predators in the various food chains and serve to keep Nature in balance.

With the decline of so many major fisheries in the world, sharks are being exploited more as a source of food today. The demand for shark fins for the use in the preparation of soup in the Orient continues unabated. As a result, the populations of commercially important sharks are now seriously reduced. Because sharks have relatively few young, and most grow slowly, their populations can be quickly depleted by overfishing.

Sharks differ in many ways from bony fishes. Their skeleton is cartilage, not bone. The jaws of sharks may seem as hard as bone, but it is only calcified cartilage. There are 5 to 7 gill openings on each side of the head of sharks, compared to a single one for bony fishes. Most sharks have a spiracle, which is a rudimentary gill opening found behind or below the eye. In bottom-dwelling sharks and rays, it is functional as the incurrent opening for respiratory water. The skin of shark is rough to the touch, due to the presence of numerous, small, dermal denticles which are close-set but not overlapping like the scales of most bony fishes. The mouth of most sharks is ventral on the head, thus the snout is overhanging. The teeth are modified, enlarged dermal denticles with a pulp cavity, dentine and a thin layer of hard, enamel-like vitrodentine. The teeth vary greatly in structure among the different species of sharks. Some teeth are sharp and blade-like, with or without serrations; others long and raptorial; and still others molariform for crushing mollusks and other hard-shelled invertebrates. When teeth are broken or worn, they are replaced from intact rows behind. Sharks lack a swimbladder, the hydrostatic organ of bony fishes. To partially offset the greater density of their bodies than seawater, sharks have a very large liver containing much oil. Also they swim with pectoral fins outstretched and angled to give them lift.

All sharks have internal fertilization; the intromittent organ of the male is the pair of claspers, one developing along the medial edge of each pelvic fin (thus the sex of sharks is easily determined externally). Some sharks are oviparous; they lay eggs in leathery cases. Most sharks are ovoviviparous; the eggs develop within the uterus. The requiem sharks (Carcharhinidae, except the Tiger Shark) and the hammerheads (Sphrynidae) are viviparous; the embryos are nourished by a placenta-like organ of the female. Most sharks have very few young, often only one or two (the Blue Shark and the Tiger Shark are exceptional in giving birth to as many as 80 and 135 pups, respectively, at one time). The intestine of sharks is very different from that of other vertebrates. It contains the spiral valve, much like an enclosed spiral staircase; indigestible items like squid beaks cannot easily pass through the intestine; from time to time a shark will regurgitate such items from its stomach.

Sharks have exceptional sensory systems. Well known is their keen olfaction which can detect attracting substances such as blood in minute quantities. Most sharks feed mainly at dusk or night (but may feed opportunistically during daylight hours); therefore their eyes are adapted to low levels of illumination. They have a tapetum lucidum behind the retina which reflects light (like a cat's eye at night); light passes through the light-receptor cells of the retina and is reflected back, thus doubling the stimulus. The highly developed lateralis system of sharks, a complex set of canals on the head and one along the side of the body with pores connecting to the surface, enables them to detect low frequency vibrations at considerable distances. Thus they are aware of the movements of prey or predators that they may not see. The pit organs in the snout, termed ampullae of Lorenzini, have been shown to act as electroreceptors. A shark is therefore able to detect the weak electromagnetic field around a sleeping fish at night.

About 40 species of sharks are known from Hawaiian waters, but 20 of these occur only in deep water. The six that are most apt to be encountered by divers or snorkelers are illustrated and discussed below.

Of greatest concern to all who venture into the sea is the threat of being bitten by a shark. However, as noted by many authors, shark attack as a cause of death in the world is negligible compared, for example, to automobile accidents. Even lightning causes more deaths than sharks. Between 1779 and 1992, 101 shark attacks have been recorded for the islands, of which 44 were fatal (although nine of the fatalities are believed to have been due to drowning or other causes). Two species of sharks in Hawaiian waters should be regarded as very dangerous, the Great White Shark (*Carcharodon carcharias*) and the Tiger Shark (*Galeocerdo cuvier*). The Great White Shark is rare in Hawai'i. The Tiger Shark, although rarely seen, is undoubtedly responsible for most of the attacks on humans in Hawaiian waters. Nevertheless, most encounters by divers with the Tiger Shark have been uneventful except for the fright they must have elicited in the divers.

REQUIEM SHARKS (CARCHARHINIDAE)

This large family consists of 12 genera and 49 species, mainly of tropical seas. It is the most important family of sharks from the standpoint of abundance, impact on marine communities, and commercial use. These sharks feed mainly on bony fishes, but also on octopuses, squids, shrimps, and sea birds. The larger species prey upon smaller sharks, rays, sea turtles, and marine mammals, in addition to bony fishes. Eleven species occur in Hawai'i; the following four are most often seen by divers.

GRAY REEF SHARK   manō   *Carcharhinus amblyrhynchos* (Bleeker, 1856)
Trailing edge of caudal fin black; no ridge on back between dorsal fins. Attains about 6 feet (180 cm).
Dangerous to spearfishermen. Should not be approached if displaying threat behavior (exaggerated slow
sinuous swimming with pectoral fins lowered). Indo-Pacific, usually on coral reefs in clear water.

GALAPAGOS SHARK   manō   *Carcharhinus galapagensis* (Snodgrass & Heller, 1905)
No conspicuous markings on fins; a low ridge on back between dorsal fins. To about 11.5 feet (350 cm).
Circumglobal in tropical and subtropical seas, especially around oceanic islands; common in the North-
western Hawaiian Islands; a dangerous shark.

BLACKTIP REEF SHARK   Manō pā'ele   *Carcharhinus melanopterus* (Quoy & Gaimard, 1824)
Brownish gray to yellowish brown with conspicuous black tips on all fins; no interdorsal ridge. Largest, 6 feet (180 cm). Indo-Pacific; generally found inshore, often in very shallow water. Ordinarily timid, but has bitten the feet or legs of persons wading on reef or sand flats.

SANDBAR SHARK   manō   *Carcharhinus plumbeus* (Nardo, 1827)
No distinctive markings on fins; first dorsal fin very large and erect. Reaches 8 feet (240 cm). Cosmopolitan in tropical to warm temperate seas, especially continental shelf localities. Not yet implicated in attack on man but potentially dangerous.

WHITETIP REEF SHARK   manō lālakeā   *Triaenodon obesus* (Rüppell, 1837)
Conspicuous white tips on dorsal and caudal fins; usually a few dark gray spots on body; snout short; body slender. Reaches 5.75 feet (175 cm). Tropical and subtropical Indo-Pacific and eastern Pacific. Often seen at rest in caves or beneath ledges by day; feeds mainly on reef fishes, occasionally on octopuses.

HAMMERHEAD SHARKS (SPHYRNIDAE)

The sharks of this family are unmistakable with the blade-like lateral extensions of their head. This unusual head shape spreads the eyes and olfactory organs farther apart; it also serves as a forward rudder, making these sharks highly maneuverable. Viviparous. A few attacks on humans are documented, but the responsible sharks were not identified as to species. Nine different species of hammerheads are known, all in the genus *Sphyrna*, but only one is positively recorded from Hawaiian waters.

SCALLOPED HAMMERHEAD   **manō kihikihi**   *Sphyrna lewini* (Griffith & Smith, 1834)
Anterior margin of head broadly convex with a prominent median indentation and 2 lesser indentations on either side. Attains 13 feet (400 cm). Worldwide in tropical to warm temperate seas. Feeds mainly on fishes, including other sharks and stingrays, and octopuses and squids. Females tend to go to calm bays to have their pups.

RAYS

Rays are characterized by their flattened form. The enlarged laterally expanded pectoral fins are fused with the body to form the disk; the five (rarely six) pairs of gill openings are ventral on the disk. Respiratory water is taken into the spiracles (an opening behind each eye) and passed out the gill openings. The mouth is ventral, the teeth generally flat and pavement-like. The rays share many of the general features listed above for sharks. Seven different families of rays are known to have a long venomous spine or spines on their tail bearing numerous small barbs on each side. The pain from wounds delivered by these spines is excruciating; deaths have been reported. Immediate soaking of a wounded limb in water as hot as can be endured helps to alleviate the pain. Rays often bury in the sand or mud with only their eyes and spiracles showing. They feed mainly on shellfish and worms, and occasionally on small burrowing fishes that they excavate from the sediment. Rays are ovoviviparous; the nutrition for the developing eggs is initially from yolk, but later from albuminous fluid secreted from vascular filaments which line the uterine wall.

STINGRAYS (DASYATIDAE)

These rays have the head as well as the body imperceptibly fused with the broad pectoral fins to form a disk which varies from nearly circular to rhomboidal in shape, often broader than long. The tail is slender without any fins (although folds of skin are present on the tail of some species); one or more strongly serrate, dangerously venomous spines are located dorsally near the base of the tail. The dorsal surface often has bony tubercles, particularly in a median zone. More than 60 species of stingrays are known in the world, but only three occur in Hawaiian waters: the pelagic *Dasyatis violacea*, *D. brevis* (*D. hawaiiensis is* a synonym) with a tail less than 1.5 times the disk length and bearing high dorsal and ventral cutaneous folds, and *D. latus* (shown below). Some stingrays reach enormous size, to over 6.5 feet (2 m) in width and a weight of 140 pounds (63.5 kg). The larger rays are able to excavate large craters in sand bottoms in quest of the animals such as mollusks and worms that live beneath the surface.

BROAD STINGRAY   lupe   *Dasyatis latus* (Garman, 1880)
Disc quadrangular, about one-fourth wider than long; tail more than twice length of disk, with a cutaneous fold only on ventral side. Attains a width of at least 2 feet (61 cm). Known only from Hawai'i and Taiwan. Not often seen in Hawai'i.

EAGLERAYS (MYLIOBATIDAE)

The eaglerays have the head distinct from the disk, with the eyes oriented more laterally than dorsally; the disc is at least 1.6 times broader than long, the outer corners acutely pointed; the tail is long and whip-like with a small dorsal fin near the base; one to several venomous spines may be present on the basal part of the tail. The teeth are flat, plate-like, and hexagonal. Eagle rays feed mainly on hard-shelled mollusks and crustaceans. The mollusk shells are crushed in the powerful jaws, and the shell fragments ejected from the mouth. The Spotted Eagleray is the only representative of the family in Hawaiian waters.

SPOTTED EAGLERAY   **hīhīmanu**   *Aetobatis narinari* (Euphrasen, 1790)
Disk dark gray to black dorsally with white spots or rings, its width 1.7-1.8 times the length; tail very long, as much as 3 times disk width, with one to five venomous spines near its base. Largest recorded, 7.5 feet (230 cm) in width. Cosmopolitan in warm seas. Very active; sometimes leaps free of the surface.

MANTA RAYS (MOBULIDAE)

This family consists of two genera, *Mobula* (common name, devilfishes) with nine species in the world (only a single record from Hawai'i), and *Manta* with an unknown number. Although many believe there is more than one kind of manta, most authors are conservative and recognize only the single species illustrated below. Mantas and devilfishes feed on zooplankton, hence are not bottom-dwelling. Like their relatives the eaglerays, they have a disk that is much wider than long, with pointed tips; the head is broad, with a pair of unique cephalic flaps, one on each side at the front, which are used to direct food organisms into the mouth; the flaps are coiled into a tight spiral when not feeding.

MANTA   **hahalua**   *Manta birostris* Walbaum, 1792
Dark gray to black dorsally, sometimes with whitish areas, and white ventrally, often with dark blotches; disk 2.2 times wider than long. Reported to a width of 23 feet (7 m). Occurs in all tropical and subtropical seas (if there is but one species of the genus). Often accompanied by the remora *Remorina albescens*.

BONY FISHES (OSTEICHTHYES)

There are two classes of fishes represented in Hawaiʻi, the cartilaginous sharks and rays (Chondrichthyes) and the bony fishes (Actinopterygii). As their name implies, the bony fishes have a bony skeleton. Another obvious external distinction is having a single gill opening on each side instead of the usual five for sharks and rays.

All but very few of the living bony fishes that occur in the sea are classified in the Teleostei. As mentioned, the order in which the fishes are presented herein is phylogenetically by family, meaning beginning with families having characters considered primitive. Among these characteristics for bony fishes are the low position of the pectoral fins on the side of the body; the origin of the pelvic fins in the posterior abdominal position; and the lack of true spines in the fins. The first two families discussed below and the eel families have a curious, ribbon-like, transparent leptocephalus larva which becomes smaller when it transforms to a juvenile.

TENPOUNDERS (ELOPIDAE)

This family, also known by the popular name ladyfishes, consists of a single genus, *Elops*. The species are regarded as among the most primitive of living teleost fishes. Their pelvic fins are near the middle of the body, with 12-16 soft rays and no spines; they have 63-79 vertebrae and small scales (up to 120 in the lateral line); the tail is forked (also true of the leptocephalus larval stage, in contrast to the leptocephali of eels which lack a caudal fin). Tenpounders are hard-fighting gamefishes that often leap when hooked. Although tasty, they are not often eaten because of the numerous small bones in the flesh. Euryhaline (i.e. they tolerate a wide range of salinity.)

HAWAIIAN TENPOUNDER   **awaʻaua**   *Elops hawaiensis* Regan, 1909.
Silvery with an elongate compressed body, very large mouth, and a single spineless dorsal fin. Hawaiian angling record, 41 inches (105 cm), 12 lbs, 6 oz (5.6 kg). Central and western Pacific; occurs along sandy shores and in shallow brackish areas; feeds on fishes and crustaceans.

BONEFISHES (ALBULIDAE)

Like the tenpounders, the bonefishes are very primitive, lacking spines in the fins, having the pectoral fins low on the body, and the pelvic fins far back in the abdominal position. Also their late larval stage is the ribbon-like transparent leptocephalus with a forked caudal fin. Adults are most distinctive in their long conical snout overhanging the ventral mouth. Until recently it was believed there was a single circumtropical species of bonefish in the world, *Albula vulpes*, but it is now known that there are five: two in the Indo-Pacific (*Albula glossodonta* and *A. argentea*), two in the western Atlantic, and one in the eastern Atlantic. Bonefishes are famous as gamefishes [the world angling record, 19 lbs. (8.6 kg.)], but they are not often eaten. Their common name is derived from the numerous small bones in the flesh. They feed mainly on small mollusks, worms, and crustaceans that live beneath the surface of sand; their teeth are small, those on the palate and floor of the mouth molari-form for crushing the hard parts of their prey. Both Indo-Pacific species occur in Hawai'i. They are difficult to distinguish when seen in life or from underwater photographs, but may be fully separated by vertebral counts (65-69 for *argentea* and 70-75 for *glossodonta*); also *argentea* has a larger mouth, the upper jaw 2.6-2.9 in head length, a more pointed lower jaw, and there is no blackish spot on the underside of the tip of the snout.

SMALLMOUTH BONEFISH   'ō'iō   *Albula glossodonta* (Forsskål, 1775)
Silvery, with a small chevron-shaped blackish spot ventrally on snout tip (may be lost in larger fish); upper jaw 3.0-3.2 in head length. Attains about 28 inches (71 cm). Indo-Pacific; occurs on sand flats of lagoons and bays. Sometimes seen in small aggregations.

MORAY EELS (MURAENIDAE)

The moray eel family is one of 15 families of true eels. The most obvious feature of eels are the very elongate body; lack of pelvic fins, a very small gill opening, and the caudal fin, if present, is joined with the dorsal and anal fins. Morays lack pectoral fins and scales; they have a large mouth with impressive dentition. Most species, such as those of the largest genus *Gymnothorax,* have long fang-like teeth, but some such as the species of *Echidna* and *Gymnomuraena* have mainly nodular or molariform teeth. The species with long canines feed mainly on reef fishes, occasionally on crustaceans and octopuses; those with blunt teeth feed primarily on crustaceans, especially crabs. Morays occasionally bite divers (the author has been bitten nine times), but usually this is a result of placing one's hand into a hole or crevice in the reef without knowing that a moray is lurking there. A human hand in a dark hole in the reef might well be mistaken by a moray for an octopus. Morays are tamed at some popular dive sites; they are hand-fed and may be handled; however, divers who do this are sometimes bitten. Recent research has shown that many morays are hermaphroditic, starting mature life as males and changing sex later to females; a few are synchronous hermaphrodites (male and female at the same time). Morays may exhibit considerable variation in color pattern, not only with growth but also among individuals the same size. There are 38 species of morays in Hawai'i; among shore fishes, only the wrasse family has more species in the islands.

SNOWFLAKE MORAY   **puhi kāpā**   *Echidna nebulosa* (Ahl, 1798)
White with two rows of large dendritic black blotches containing small yellow spots; small black spots among the large black blotches, becoming more numerous and irregularly linear with growth; no canine teeth. Attains 28 inches (71 cm). Indo-Pacific and tropical eastern Pacific in shallow water. Feeds mainly on crabs. More inclined than most morays to swim in the open.

DRAGON MORAY **puhi kauila** *Enchelycore pardalis* (Temminck & Schlegel, 1846)
Brownish orange with numerous round white spots and small black spots; jaws curved and cannot completely close; many large canine teeth; posterior nostrils long and tubular. To 36 inches (92 cm). Indo-Pacific; more common in the Northwestern Hawaiian Islands than the main islands.

VIPER MORAY **puhi kauila** *Enchelynassa canina* (Quoy & Gaimard, 1824)
Dark brown; jaws close only at tips, canine teeth very long; anterior nostrils back from snout tip, with a long fringed posterior flap; posterior nostrils large and oval, well before eyes. Reported to 5 feet (150 cm). Central and western Pacific, and tropical eastern Pacific. The awesome dentition commands respect.

ZEBRA MORAY **puhi** *Gymnomuraena zebra* (Shaw & Nodder, 1797)
Dark brown to dark orangish brown, encircled by many narrow pale yellowish bars; numerous molariform teeth in jaws and on palate. Reported to 5 feet (150 cm), but any over 4 feet are exceptional. Indo-Pacific and tropical eastern Pacific. Feeds principally on crabs.

WHITEMARGIN MORAY   puhi   *Gymnothorax albimarginatus* (Temminck & Schlegel, 1846)   Brown, the fins with a white margin; sensory pores on jaws in a white spot; body slender; some teeth finely serrate. Attains 40 inches (1 m). Hawai'i to western Pacific, in coral reefs. A colleague reported severe pain from a bite, suggesting a venom (known for other morays with serrate teeth).

STOUT MORAY   puhi   *Gymnothorax eurostus* (Abbott, 1861)
Color variable, but generally light brown, darker posteriorly, with numerous small pale spots; black spots on about anterior half of body arranged in approximate vertical rows. Largest, 22.5 inches (60 cm). Indo-Pacific and eastern Pacific; antitropical. The most common inshore moray in Hawai'i, but not often seen.

YELLOWMARGIN MORAY   puhi paka   *Gymnothorax flavimarginatus* (Rüppell, 1830)
Yellowish, densely mottled with dark brown, with a black spot on gill opening and a yellow-green margin posteriorly on fins. Reaches 48 inches (120 cm). Indo-Pacific and tropical eastern Pacific; one of the most common morays in Hawai'i and the one most often tamed.

GIANT MORAY   puhi *Gymnothorax javanicus* (Bleeker, 1859)
Light brown with large irregular dark brown blotches and numerous small dark brown spots; gill opening in a large black spot. Reaches about 8 feet (245 cm); the largest species of the genus in the Indo-Pacific; occurs in coral reefs. Rare in the Hawaiian Islands, but common at Johnston Island.

DWARF MORAY   puhi *Gymnothorax melatremus* Schultz, 1953
Bright yellow to brown, sometimes with dark markings; gill opening in a black spot; a black rim around eye; iris blue with a black bar. Largest specimen, 10.2 inches (26 cm). Indo-Pacific; common in Hawai'i but rarely seen.

WHITEMOUTH MORAY   puhi 'ōni'o *Gymnothorax meleagris* (Shaw & Nodder, 1795)
Brown to orangish brown with numerous dark-edged round white spots; tip of tail white; gill opening in a blackish spot; inside of mouth white. Reaches about 40 inches (1 m). Indo-Pacific and Galapagos Islands. Seen by divers on Hawaiian reefs more often than other morays.

YELLOWMOUTH MORAY   puhi   *Gymnothorax nudivomer* (Playfair & Günther, 1867)
Light brown anteriorly with numerous tiny irregular white spots; dark brown posteriorly, the spots larger toward the tail, rimmed with dark brown, and more widely spaced ; inside of mouth yellow. Reaches 40 inches (1 m). Hawai'i to East Africa, usually in more than 100 feet (30.5 m). Secretes a skin toxin.

BANDED MORAY   puhi 'ou   *Scuticaria okinawae* (Jordan & Snyder, 1901)
Light grayish brown with 16-21 dark brown bars, those posterior to anus circling body and fins, some on trunk not meeting ventrally (bars less distinct on larger eels); top of head yellow; a dark brown spot at corner of mouth. Reaches 32 inches (81 cm). Indo-Pacific. Nocturnal.

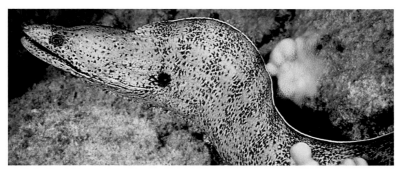

STEINDACHNER'S MORAY   puhi   *Gymnothorax steindachneri* Jordan & Evermann, 1903.
Light brown to nearly white, with irregular small dark brown spots, often forming obscure bars; a dark brown blotch at gill opening, and a smaller one at corner of mouth. Attains 34 inches (87 cm). Known only from Hawai'i; common in shallow water in the Northwestern Hawaiian Islands, generally in 100 feet (30.5 m) or more in the main islands.

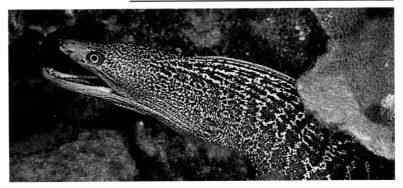

UNDULATED MORAY **puhi lau milo** *Gymnothorax undulatus* (Lacepède, 1803)
Pale yellowish with large and small, irregular, close-set, dark brown spots, the large spots tending to
form irregular bars posteriorly on body which extend into fins; top of head often yellow-green. To 3.5
feet (107 cm). Indo-Pacific and tropical eastern Pacific; moderately common in the Hawaiian Islands.
Primarily nocturnal. More prone to bite than most morays.

BENNETT'S MORAY **puhi** *Scuticaria bennettii* (Günther, 1870)
Uniform brown; body very elongate; tail (i.e. body posterior to anus) about one-third total length; fins
not apparent; posterior nostril over front edge of eye. Reaches at least 37 inches (94 cm). Hawai'i and
Tahiti to Mauritius; rarely seen by day; probably nocturnal.

TIGER MORAY **puhi** *Scuticaria tigrina* (Lesson, 1828)
Pale yellowish to light brown with roundish dark brown spots of variable size (small anteriorly on head);
body very elongate; tail less than one-third total length; dorsal and anal fins rudimentary, at end of tail.
Attains about 4 feet (122 cm). Indo-Pacific and tropical eastern Pacific; nocturnal. *Uropterygius polyspilus*
similar in color, but anus near middle of body.

SNAKE EELS AND WORM EELS (OPHICHTHIDAE)

This is the largest and most diverse family of eels; 55 genera and more than 250 species are currently known. All are very elongate, some extremely so; the body is usually cylindrical, at least anteriorly; the posterior nostrils open inside the mouth or through a valve in the upper lip; the numerous branchiostegal rays overlap ventrally. There are two subfamilies, the snake eels (Ophichthinae), characterized by a sharply pointed tail without a caudal fin, and the worm eels (Myrophinae) with a small caudal fin at the tip of the tail. Snake eels are rarely seen by divers because they are secretive in reefs or are buried in the sand or mud; those that live in sediment use the tip of the tail for burrowing. Only 16 species are reported from the Hawaiian Islands; the three most apt to be observed by divers (all in the Ophichthinae) are presented below.

CROCODILE SNAKE EEL   **puhi**   *Brachysomophis crocodilinus* (Bennett, 1831).
Light brown dorsally, sparsely dotted with dark brown, shading to pale yellowish below; lateral-line pores in a small brown spot; head usually red with white markings; dorsal fin blackish with white margin; eye far forward on head. Reaches 40 inches (1 m). Indo-Pacific. Lives under sand except for upper head; ambushes fishes and crustaceans that venture near. *B. henshawi* Jordan & Snyder is a synonym.

FRECKLED SNAKE EEL   **puhi**   *Callechelys lutea* Snyder, 1904.
White to pale yellowish with numerous scattered black spots, mostly small and oval in shape; body very elongate and somewhat compressed; no pectoral fins; dorsal fin high, its origin nearly to above corner of mouth. Reaches at least 3 feet (92 cm). Hawaiian Islands; occasionally seen with head protruding nearly vertically from sand. Similar to *C. marmorata* (Bleeker) from elsewhere in the Indo-Pacific.

MAGNIFICENT SNAKE EEL **puhi lā'au** *Myrichthys magnificus* (Abbott, 1861).
White with large round black spots, more numerous in larger individuals; body very elongate, compressed posteriorly; dorsal-fin origin well before gill openings; pectoral fins shorter than their base. Largest, 30.6 inches (78 cm). Hawai'i and Johnston Island. The similar *M. maculosus* occurs in the rest of the Indo-Pacific. It has 185-199 vertebrae compared to 177-183 for *M. magnificus*.

CONGER EELS (CONGRIDAE)

Conger eels have a nearly cylindrical body (becoming compressed posteriorly), well-developed pectoral fins, a moderately large gill opening on lower half of body, the upper end just in front of pectoral-fin base, a complete lateral line with distinct pores, and no scales; the lips have a free margin on the side. Most of the species occur in deep water. Four shallow-water Hawaiian representatives are presented below. Congers are often called White Eels in Hawai'i.

LARGE-EYE CONGER **puhi** *Ariosoma marginatum* (Vaillant & Sauvage, 1875)
Light gray-brown with silvery reflections; a broad pale-edged dark bar behind eye; a narrow blackish margin on median fins; eye large, about equal to snout length. Attains 15 inches (38 cm). Hawaiian Islands; sand-dwelling from the shallows to 1600 feet (490 m); may be seen at night with head protruding obliquely from sand. *A. bowersi* (Jenkins) is a synonym.

MUSTACHE CONGER   **puhi ūhā**   *Conger cinereus* Rüppell, 1830
Brownish gray with a blackish streak below eye parallel to upper lip; prominent black margins on median fins; often a large blackish area on pectoral fins. Reaches 4.5 feet (137 cm). Indo-Pacific; subspecifically different in Hawai'i. Nocturnal; displays a strong dark-barred pattern at night. Preys on crustaceans and fishes. More appreciated as a food fish in Hawai'i than moray eels.

HAWAIIAN GARDEN EEL   **puhi**   *Gorgasia hawaiiensis* Randall & Chess, 1980
Light greenish gray with numerous small brownish yellow spots; body extremely elongate, the depth 64-86 times in length; pectoral fins smaller than eye. Reaches 2 feet (61 cm). Hawaiian Islands. Occurs in colonies in burrows on sand bottom in 35-175 feet (11-53 m). Feeds diurnally on individual animals of the plankton, hence usually found where there is appreciable current.

BARRED CONGER   *Poeciloconger fasciatus* Günther, 1871.
Adults whitish with about 12 irregular double dark brown bars on body and numerous small dark brown spots on head; dorsal fin with large dark brown spots and bars; juveniles with fewer bars and spots; caudal fin abbreviated, and terminal caudal region stiff. Reaches at least 2 feet (60 cm). Known to date from Madagascar, Indonesia, Marshall Islands, Hawai'i, and Tahiti. Lives in sand for which the stiff caudal region is an adaptation, for rapid backward burrowing.

HERRINGS AND SARDINES (CLUPEIDAE)

Fishes of this family are small, silvery, with a single short dorsal fin near the middle of the body, no spines, no lateral line, pectoral fins low, pelvic fins in a posterior abdominal position, and a forked caudal fin. They are nearly always encountered in schools; most feed on plankton. Four marine species occur in the Hawaiian Islands; two are native, and two were introduced. The Redeye Roundherring (*Etrumeus teres*) is rare in Hawai'i; it grows to nearly 12 inches (30 cm). The Marquesan Sardine (*Sardinella marquesensis*) was brought to Hawai'i from the Marquesas between 1955 and 1959 as a baitfish for tuna; it never became abundant.

GOLDSPOT SARDINE   *Herklotsichthys quadrimaculatus* (Rüppell, 1837)
Blue-green on back, shading to silvery on sides and ventrally, with an orange-yellow spot behind upper end of gill opening and another below it. Reaches 5.5 inches (14 cm). Indo-Pacific. Unintentionally introduced to the Hawaiian Islands from the Marshall Islands in 1972.

DELICATE ROUNDHERRING   **pihā**   *Spratelloides delicatulus* (Bennett, 1831)
Blue on back, silvery below; two dark streaks on base of caudal fin; a single W-shaped scute (enlarged scale) in front of pelvic fins. Attains 3.3 inches (8.4 cm). Indo-Pacific; an inshore species that may be seen in small schools over reefs.

ANCHOVIES (ENGRAULIDAE)

The anchovies share the primitive characters listed above for the clupeid fishes such as a single dorsal fin, no spines in fins, etc. They are readily distinguished by their rounded overhanging snout and slender lower jaw. Anchovies occur in dense schools; they feed by swimming open-mouth through concentrations of planktonic organisms which are strained on their numerous slender gill rakers. Only two species are known from Hawaiian waters, the common Hawaiian Anchovy and the Buccaneer Anchovy (*Encrasicholina punctifer*); the latter is wide-ranging and usually found offshore.

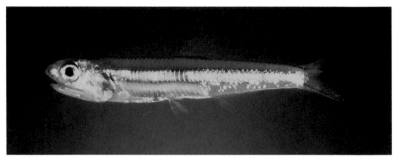

HAWAIIAN ANCHOVY   **nehu**   *Encrasicholina purpurea* (Fowler, 1900)
Greenish on back with a broad lateral silvery stripe; belly rounded, usually without prepelvic scutes (*E. punctifer* has 3-6 needle-like scutes before the pelvic fins). Attains 2 inches (5.1 cm). Hawaiian Islands; occurs inshore, often in brackish bays. Important as a tuna baitfish.

MILKFISH FAMILY (CHANIDAE)

MILKFISH   **awa**   *Chanos chanos* Forsskål, 1775
Only species of the family. Silvery; a single dorsal fin; no spines; caudal fin very large and forked; pectoral fins low on side, and pelvic fins posterior to middle of body; scales very small; lateral line on midside. Reports of 6 feet (1.8 m) may be exaggerated, but probably attains 5 feet (1.5 m). Indo-Pacific and tropical eastern Pacific. Important food fish; reared in ponds in Asia and by ancient Hawaiians.

LIZARDFISHES (SYNODONTIDAE)

Aptly named for their reptile-like head, lizardfishes have a large mouth and numerous needle-like teeth; even the tongue has teeth. The body is cylindrical and moderately elongate. There are no spines in the fins; the single dorsal fin is relatively high with 10-14 rays; it is followed by the small so-called adipose fin; the caudal fin is forked; the pelvic fins are large with 8-9 rays. Species of three shallow-water genera occur in Hawaiian waters; those of the genus *Saurida* have numerous small teeth on the side of the jaws which are visible when the mouth is closed; the species of the large genus *Synodus* lack such teeth. Lizardfishes are usually found on sand or mud bottoms; they are able to bury themselves quickly in the sediment. All are voracious carnivores, darting rapidly upward to seize their prey of small fishes, shrimps, or squids. Seventeen species occur in the Hawaiian Islands, some of which are found only in deeper-than-diving depths.

ORANGEMOUTH LIZARDFISH   'ulae   *Saurida flamma* Waples, 1982
A series of slightly oblique, narrow, reddish to dark brown bars on side of body; three dusky to black blotches dorsally on posterior half of body, the largest just behind dorsal fin; side of jaws bright orange or red with narrow white bars; lateral-line scales 53-54 (usually 54). Reaches 13 inches (33 cm). Hawai'i, Austral Islands, and Pitcairn; usually found in reef habitats.

SLENDER LIZARDFISH   'ulae   *Saurida gracilis* Quoy & Gaimard, 1824
Mottled dorsally, white ventrally, with a series of near-vertical blackish bars on side of body and three diffuse blackish blotches dorsally on posterior half of body, the largest behind dorsal fin; lateral-line scales 49-52. Attains 11 inches (28 cm). Indo-Pacific; usually on sand or silty sand near protected reefs.

NEBULOUS LIZARDFISH   'ulae   *Saurida nebulosa* Valenciennes, 1849.
Color very similar to that of *S. gracilis*; lateral-line scales 50-52; best distinguished by shorter pectoral fins (the tips 4-6 scale rows from origin of dorsal fin; 2-3 rows for *S. gracilis*). Largest, 8 inches (20 cm). Indo-Pacific; usually in shallow turbid areas on silty sand.

TWOSPOT LIZARDFISH   'ulae   *Synodus binotatus* Schultz, 1953
Two small black spots on tip of snout; 3.5 rows of scales above lateral line; lateral-line scales 53-55; pectoral fins reach beyond a line connecting origins of dorsal and pelvic fins. Attains about 7 inches (18 cm). Indo-Pacific; few records from more than 65 feet (20 m).

CAPRICORN LIZARDFISH   'ulae   *Synodus capricornis* Cressey & Randall, 1978
A series of 7 near-round dark brown spots with orange or red centers along lateral line; about 15 narrow reddish to orangish bars on lower half of body; scales above lateral line 5.5; lateral-line scales 65-66. Reaches 9 inches (23 cm). Known only from Easter Island, Pitcairn, and Hawai'i; therefore an apparent example of antitropical distribution. Generally found in more than 65 feet (20 m).

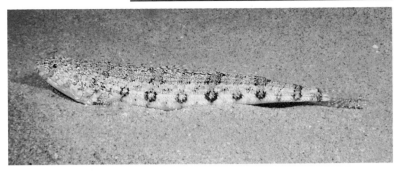

CLEARFIN LIZARDFISH 'ulae *Synodus dermatogenys* Fowler, 1912
A series of 8 or 9 dark blotches, often with pale centers, along lateral line, narrower than pale intervening spaces; 6 small black spots on tip of snout; 5.5 scales above lateral line; lateral-line scales 59-62. Largest, 9 inches (23 cm); Indo-Pacific; on sand or rubble near coral reefs.

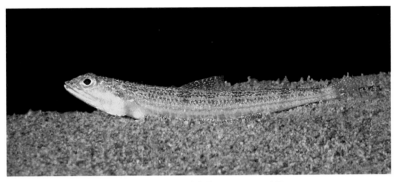

LOBEL'S LIZARDFISH 'ulae *Synodus lobeli* Waples & Randall, 1988
A narrow midlateral yellow stripe on body faintly edged in grayish blue; back above with fine irregular dark brown markings and a narrow blue stripe; body slender; scales above lateral line 3.5; lateral-line scales 53-55. Largest in Hawai'i, 5.5 inches (14 cm). Hawai'i and Japan; collected in Hawai'i in 105 feet (32 m) on sand well away from reefs.

ULAE 'ulae *Synodus ulae* Schultz, 1953
A series of 8 roundish dark blotches with pale centers along lateral line as wide or wider than pale inter-spaces; numerous small dark blotches on head; scales above lateral line 5.5; lateral-line scales 63-66. Attains 13 inches (33 cm). Hawai'i and Japan; the most common lizardfish on shallow sandy areas in Hawai'i. Spawning occurs in pairs shortly after sunset, following an upward dash up to 13 feet (4 m).

REEF LIZARDFISH **'ulae** *Synodus variegatus* (Lacepède, 1803)
A narrow orange-red to greenish gray midlateral stripe containing 7 or 8 darker spots a little wider than stripe; scales above lateral line 5.5; lateral-line scales 61-63; scales on cheek behind mouth extend to edge of preopercle. Largest, 10.5 inches (27 cm). Indo-Pacific; a very common species. Seen more often at rest on coral reefs or rocky bottoms than any other lizardfish.

SNAKEFISH **wele'ā** *Trachinocephalus myops* (Forster & Schneider, 1801)
Body with narrow pale blue and yellow stripes; a black spot at upper end of gill opening; snout short, equal to or shorter than eye diameter; mouth strongly oblique. Reaches 13 inches (33 cm). Indo-Pacific and Atlantic in tropical to warm temperate seas; on sand bottom from the shallows to 1300 feet (400 m); usually seen buried in sand except for its eyes.

BROTULAS AND CUSK EELS (OPHIDIIDAE)

These fishes are moderately elongate with broad-based dorsal and anal fins that are confluent with the caudal fin; pelvic fins are absent or consist of one or two filamentous rays; some species have barbels around the mouth similar to those of catfishes. Most species occur in deep water; the few in shallow water are cryptic and rarely seen except at night. Two species of *Brotula* are known from Hawai'i; the common *B. multibarbata* and *B. townsendi;* the latter has a small eye, its diameter less than the fleshy interorbital space.

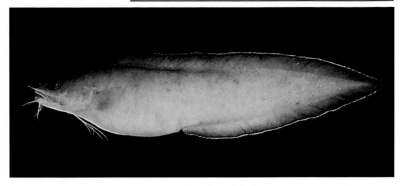

LARGE-EYE BROTULA **palahoana** *Brotula multibarbata* Temminck & Schlegel, 1846
Orangish brown with 3 pairs of pale barbels on snout and 3 pairs on chin; dorsal and anal fins with numerous soft rays, nearly uniform in height; pelvic fins filamentous, the outer half bifurcate. Reaches 2 feet (60 cm). Indo-Pacific. Nocturnal; difficult to photograph because it quickly seeks shelter when a light is shined in its direction.

FROGFISHES (ANTENNARIIDAE)

The bizarre fishes of this family are often called anglerfishes, but this is the general common name for the 16 families of the order Lophiiformes of which the Antennariidae is one. The species of these families have the first dorsal spine modified to a lure consisting of the slender ilicium tipped with the esca (bait) which is used to attract prey. The frogfishes have a globose compressed body with a loose scaleless skin that may have wart-like protuberances or small tentacles or cirri. The mouth is very large and highly oblique to vertical. There are two more dorsal spines on the head behind the ilicium; the third spine is curved and usually broadly connected to the nape by membrane. The prehensile pectoral fins are limb-like with an "elbow" joint. The

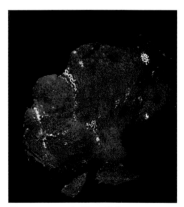

Commerson's Frogfish

gill opening is small and round, located on the basal part of the pectoral appendage or behind it. The color of frogfishes is extremely variable; they generally match their surroundings very well. If the background color is changed, they may in a few weeks dramatically change color, as from red or yellow to black. Although frogfishes are able to slowly stalk their prey of fishes or crustaceans, they usually remain stationary and lure the prey by wriggling the esca above the mouth. They can engulf fishes longer than themselves, hence not good choices for aquaria with other fishes.

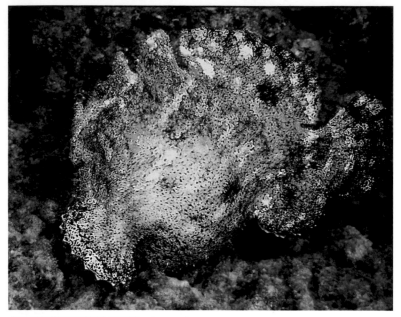

COMMERSON'S FROGFISH *Antennarius commerson* (Latreille, 1804)
Color may be yellow, red, orange, brown, gray, or black, and variously mottled; ilicium about as long as third dorsal spine and nearly twice as long as second; second dorsal spine broadly joined to head by membrane; dorsal rays usually 13; pectoral rays usually 11. Reaches 14 inches (36 cm). Indo-Pacific and tropical eastern Pacific. The most common species seen by divers in Hawai'i.

HAWAIIAN FRECKLED FROGFISH *Antennarius drombus* Jordan & Evermann, 1903
Color variable; often gray or brown with small dark blotches; ilicium about as long as second dorsal spine; second dorsal spine curved, its connecting membrane short; soft dorsal and anal fins end at base of caudal fin; dorsal rays 12; pectoral rays 12. To 4.5 inches (11.5 cm). Hawai'i; the related *A. coccineus*, with 10 pectoral rays, occurs in the rest of the Indo-Pacific region.

PAINTED FROGFISH   *Antennarius pictus* (Shaw & Nodder, 1794)
Black, yellowish, orange, rust red, or brown, usually with ocellated dark spots of different size; dark individuals often with white-tipped pectoral rays; ilicium about twice as long as second dorsal spine; membrane attaching second dorsal spine to head thin, with spinules; dorsal rays usually 12; pectoral rays usually 10. Largest, 8.3 inches (21 cm). Indo-Pacific.

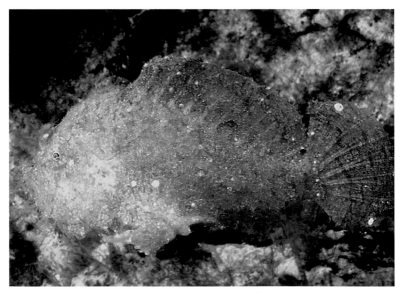

RANDALL'S FROGFISH   *Antennarius randalli* Allen, 1970
Yellowish, reddish brown, to nearly black; a blackish spot basally in dorsal fin; 2 white spots often present in caudal fin; ilicium shorter than second dorsal spine; membrane of second dorsal fin connected to third dorsal spine, and its membrane to soft dorsal fin; dorsal rays usually 12; pectoral rays 9. A small species, to 1.7 inches (4.3 cm). Easter Island and Hawai'i to western Pacific.

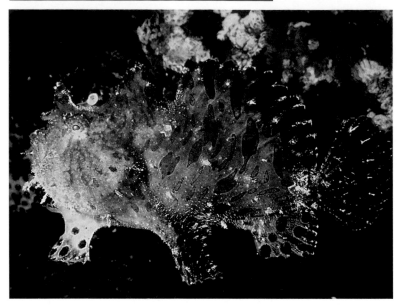

STRIATED FROGFISH   *Antennarius striatus* (Shaw & Nodder, 1794)
Typically light yellow to orangish, but may be greenish, gray, brown, nearly white or black; numerous oblique dark streaks or elongate spots; ilicium slightly longer than second dorsal spine, the esca often as 2 or 3 worm-like parts; dorsal rays 12; pectoral rays 10 or 11. Largest, 8.6 inches (22 cm). Indo-Pacific and tropical Atlantic; usually on bottoms of seagrass, algae, or sponge.

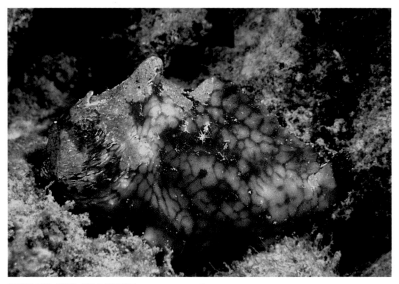

RETICULATED FROGFISH   *Antennatus tuberosus* (Cuvier, 1817)
Usually gray to yellow with a dark brown reticulum, often with whitish or pink areas on head; ilicium without an esca (bait), 1.5-2 times longer than second dorsal spine; dorsal rays usually 12; pectoral rays 10-11. Attains 3.5 inches (9 cm). Indo-Pacific, from the shallows to at least 240 feet (73 m). A coral-reef species; often shelters in branching corals.

SILVERSIDES (ATHERINIDAE)

The silversides are small slender fishes which usually form schools. They have two well-separated dorsal fins, the first of III to VIII slender flexible spines; the second dorsal and anal fins have an initial spine; the pectoral fins are high on the side of the body; there is no lateral line. Typically they have a broad silvery stripe on the side of the body. They feed on zooplankton, and, in turn, are heavily preyed upon by jacks and other roving predaceous fishes. Their eggs are large and demersal, with adhesive threads. Only a single species is found in Hawai'i.

HAWAIIAN SILVERSIDE   'iao   *Atherinomorus insularum* (Jordan & Evermann, 1903)
Greenish gray on back with a broad silvery stripe on side; tips of the forked caudal fin dusky; body robust for the family; eye large. Reaches 5 inches (13 cm). Hawaiian Islands; forms schools inshore in calm areas. Often used as a baitfish, though not as important as the **nehu**. Related to *Atherimomorus lacunosus* (Bloch & Schneider) from elsewhere in the Indo-Pacific region.

NEEDLEFISHES (BELONIDAE)

Needlefishes are very elongate with long pointed jaws bearing numerous needle-like teeth; there are no spines in the fins; the dorsal and anal fins are posterior on the body; the lateral line passes along the lower side. These fishes are surface-dwelling and protectively colored green or blue on the back and silvery below; some species have green bones. They feed mainly on small fishes. When frightened, as by a predator or approaching boat, or confused by a light at night, they may leap and skitter at the surface. People have been injured by being struck by the larger needlefishes, and fatalities have been reported. Four marine species occur in Hawaiian waters; the two presented below are the most common.

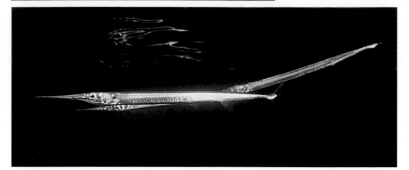

KEELTAIL NEEDLEFISH   **'aha**   *Platybelone argalus* (Lesueur, 1821)
Blue or blue-green dorsally, silvery on sides and ventrally; body and jaws extremely elongate; body width slightly greater than depth, the caudal peduncle about twice as wide as deep, with a keel on the side. Attains nearly 18 inches (45 cm). Divisible into 5 subspecies: Indo-Pacific, eastern Pacific, Arabian, and north and south Atlantic. Occurs inshore; often observed in small aggregations.

HOUNDFISH   **'aha**   *Tylosurus crocodilus* (Peron & Lesueur, 1821)
Green on the back, silvery below; a blackish keel on side of caudal peduncle; body slender in juveniles, progressively less elongate in adults; jaws relatively shorter with growth; anterior part of dorsal and anal fins elevated. The largest of the needlefishes; attains at least 53 inches (135 cm). Worldwide in warm seas, usually in coastal waters. This living javelin is a hazard to those using a light at night.

HALFBEAKS (HEMIRAMPHIDAE)

    Halfbeaks are related to the needlefishes, sharing such characters as the elongate body, no spines in fins, and lateral line low on the side of the body. They are easily distinguished by having a short triangular upper jaw and a very long slender lower jaw; the caudal fin is forked, the lower lobe longer than upper. Halfbeaks live at or near the surface and may leap clear of the sea and skip like needlefishes; two offshore species are able to glide on outstretched pectoral fins like flyingfishes. Some feed on plant material, especially floating pieces of seagrass, and others on zooplankton and small fishes. The eggs have adhesive filaments and are generally attached to floating or benthic plants. Two inshore species occur in Hawai'i.

POLYNESIAN HALFBEAK **iheihe** *Hemiramphus depauperatus* Lay & Bennett, 1839
Green on back, silvery below; tip of lower jaw red; body depth greater than base of anal fin; no scales on upper jaw; origin of dorsal fin well in advance of anal fin. Reaches at least 15 inches (38 cm). Hawaiian Islands, Line Islands, and French Polynesia.

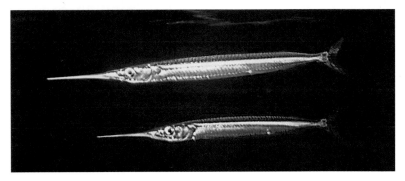

ACUTE HALFBEAK **iheihe** *Hyporhamphus acutus* (Günther, 1871)
Iridescent blue-green on back, silvery on sides and ventrally; tip of lower jaw red; body very slender; lower jaw very long, usually longer than head length; scales on upper jaw; dorsal-fin origin over anal-fin origin. Largest, 13.5 inches (34 cm). Islands of Oceania; subspecifically different in Hawai'i.

SQUIRRELFISHES AND SOLDIERFISHES (HOLOCENTRIDAE)

The fishes of this family are spiny, red or partly red, with very large eyes. They have XI or XII (usually XI) dorsal spines, IV anal spines, and the pelvic fins with I,7 rays; the caudal fin is forked; the scales are coarsely ctenoid (their edges with numerous sharp spinules); the external bones of the head have ridges and grooves, some with small spines or serrate edges; the mouth is fairly large, but the teeth are small. The family is divisible into two subfamilies, the Holocentrinae (squirrelfishes) with two Indo-Pacific genera (*Neoniphon* and *Sargocentron*), and the Myripristinae (soldierfishes) with four Indo-Pacific genera (*Myripristis, Plectrypops, Pristilepis,* and *Ostichthys*); the species of the last two genera occur in deep water. The squirrelfishes are characterized by a long sharp spine at the corner of the preopercle, which may be venomous, and a some-what pointed snout; the soldierfishes lack the spine on the preopercle or have a short broad-based one, and the snout is short and blunt. Squirrelfishes and soldierfishes are nocturnal, as their large eyes suggest. They occur on reefs, tending to hide in caves or beneath ledges by day, coming out to forage for food at night. The squirrelfishes prey mainly on benthic crustaceans, whereas the soldierfishes feed on the larger animals of the zooplankton, such as crab larvae, often well above the bottom. The general Hawaiian name for squirrelfishes is **'ala'ihi** and of the soldierfishes **'ū'ū** (though the local name **mempachi** has largely replaced it).

BRICK SOLDIERFISH   **'ū'ū**   *Myripristis amaena* (Castelnau, 1873)
Outer part of spinous dorsal fin red; no white on leading edges of fins; 32-36 lateral-line scales. Reaches 10.5 inches (26.5 cm). Appears to be confined to the islands of Oceania. Generally found inshore in less than 30 feet (9 m). *M. argyromus* Jordan & Evermann is a synonym.

BIGSCALE SOLDIERFISH   **'ū'ū**   *Myripristis berndti* Jordan & Evermann, 1903
Outer part of spinous dorsal fin orange-yellow; white on leading edges of fins; 28-31 lateral-line scales; small scales in pectoral-fin axil; lower jaw projecting. Attains 11 inches (28 cm). East Africa to the tropical eastern Pacific ; the most common soldierfish in Hawai'i in the depth range of 50-150 feet (15-46 m).

YELLOWFIN SOLDIERFISH 'ū'ū *Myripristis chryseres* Jordan & Evermann, 1903
Median and pelvic fins mainly yellow; lateral-line scales 32-38; a deep notch at front of upper jaw. Reaches 10 inches (25 cm). Wide-ranging in the Indo-Pacific region, but from scattered localities; usually found at depths greater than 100 feet (30.5 m).

EPAULETTE SOLDIERFISH 'ū'ū *Myripristis kuntee* Cuvier, 1831
A reddish brown bar from upper end of gill opening to pectoral-fin base; outer part of spinous dorsal fin yellow; leading edges of fins narrowly white; lateral-line scales 37-44. Reaches 7.5 inches (19 cm). Indo-Pacific; may be seen as solitary fish or in aggregations. *M. multiradiatus* Günther is a synonym.

WHITETIP SOLDIERFISH 'ū'ū *Myripristis vittata* Valenciennes, 1831
Orange-red without a dark brown bar at edge of gill opening; tips of dorsal spines and leading edges of fins white; lateral-line scales 35-40. Reaches 8 inches (20 cm). Indo-Pacific, generally at depths greater than 50 feet (15 m); rare in Hawai'i; first discovered at Molokini off Maui in 1990.

GOLDLINED SQUIRRELFISH   **'ala'ihi**   *Neoniphon aurolineatus* (Liénard, 1839)
Silvery pink with narrow golden yellow stripes; lateral-line scales 42-47. Attains about 9 inches (23 cm). Indo-Pacific, mainly from insular localities. Not common; generally found at depths greater than 100 feet (30.5 m). *Flammeo scythrops* Jordan & Evermann is a synonym.

SPOTFIN SQUIRRELFISH   **'ala'ihi**   *Neoniphon sammara* (Forsskål, 1775)
Silvery with narrow dark reddish stripes and a large black spot at front of dorsal fin; a red stripe on the upper side at night; lateral-line scales 38-43. Attains 12 inches (30 cm). Indo-Pacific, from the Red Sea to Hawai'i and Pitcairn Islands; common on shallow protected reefs. Feeds mainly on small crabs, shrimps, and small fishes (generally juveniles or newly settled postlarvae).

ROUGHSCALE SOLDIERFISH   **'ū'ū**   *Plectrypops lima* (Valenciennes, 1831)
Uniform red; dorsal rays XII,14-16. Maximum length 6.3 inches (16 cm). Indo-Pacific; hides in the deepest recesses of reefs by day and rarely ventures from caves at night. Difficult to photograph underwater; when illuminated, it darts for shelter. Formerly classified in *Holotrachys*.

CROWN SQUIRRELFISH   **'ala'ihi**   *Sargocentron diadema* (Lacepède, 1801)
Red with narrow silvery white stripes on body; spinous dorsal fin deep red to nearly black with a disjunct whitish stripe in lower part; the two opercular spines about equal. Reported to 6.7 inches (17 cm), but rarely exceeds 5 inches (12.5 cm). Indo-Pacific; common in the depth range of 7-100 feet (2-30.5 m).

YELLOWSTRIPED SQUIRRELFISH   **'ala'ihi**   *Sargocentron ensifer* (Jordan & Evermann, 1903) Red with narrow yellow stripes dorsally and white stripes ventrally; spinous dorsal yellow with a red margin, the first spine about as long as second. To 10 inches (25 cm). Hawai'i, Japan, South China Sea, New Caledonia, and Pitcairn, usually at depths greater than 60 feet (18 m).

PEPPERED SQUIRRELFISH   **'ala'ihi**   *Sargocentron punctatissimum* (Cuvier, 1829).
Silvery pink with red stripes, usually with a stippling of blackish pigment. Attains 5 inches (13 cm). Indo-Pacific; generally found on exposed rocky shores or reef fronts; occurs in shallower water than other squirrelfishes, sometimes in large tidepools. *Holocentrus lacteoguttatus* Cuvier is a synonym.

SABER SQUIRRELFISH   **'ala'ihi**   *Sargocentron spiniferum* (Forsskål, 1775)
Red, the edges of the scales silvery white; a large crimson spot behind eye bordered with white except ventrally; spinous dorsal solid red; 3.5 scales above lateral line (2.5 in most other species of the genus). Largest of the squirrelfishes; to 18 inches (45 cm). Indo-Pacific. The long preopercular spine is venomous. More common at Johnston Island and elsewhere in Oceania than Hawai'i.

TAHITIAN SQUIRRELFISH   **'ala'ihi**   *Sargocentron tiere* (Cuvier, 1829)
Red with silvery red stripes, those ventrally on body with blue iridescence; spinous dorsal fin short, red with white spine tips and a row of white spots. To 13 inches (33 cm). Indo-Pacific, usually from islands; occurs from the shallows to at least 65 feet (20 m). Scientific name from the Tahitian common name.

HAWAIIAN SQUIRRELFISH 'ala'ihi *Sargocentron xantherythrum* (Jordan & Evermann, 1903) Red with narrow silvery white stripes; spinous dorsal fin solid red except for white spine tips; uppermost of two opercular spines clearly longest. Attains 6.5 inches (16.5 cm). Known only from Johnston Island and the Hawaiian Islands where it is the most common squirrelfish in SCUBA-diving depths.

TRUMPETFISHES (AULOSTOMIDAE)

Trumpetfishes are very elongate with a compressed body (i.e. narrower than deep), a small mouth at the end of a long tubular snout, minute teeth, and a small barbel on the chin; there are VIII to XII slender isolated dorsal spines, followed by a normal dorsal fin; the caudal fin is rounded to rhomboid. They swim (when not in a hurry) by undulating the dorsal and anal fins which are set far back on the body. They feed mainly on fishes and shrimps by slowly moving close to the prey (often from a vertical  stance), then darting forward and sucking it in. The ventral part of the snout is membranous and elastic, thus prey with a greater body depth than the snout can be eaten. Trumpetfishes sometimes mingle with schools of plant-feeding surgeonfishes in order to approach small fishes disrupted by the school. Also they often swim alongside larger fishes, presumably to get closer to their prey. There are three species in the world, one at islands of the eastern Atlantic, one in the western Atlantic, and the third in the Pacific and Indian Oceans.

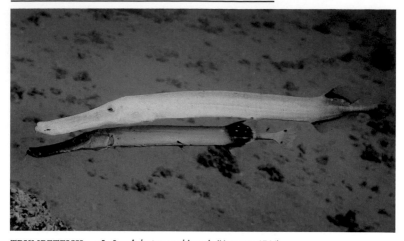

TRUMPETFISH   nūnū   *Aulostomus chinensis* (Linnaeus, 1766)
Two color forms, yellow and the more common gray-brown or orangish brown, usually with faint narrow whitish stripes, becoming blackish posteriorly with vertical rows of white spots; 2 black spots in caudal fin, 1 at base of each pelvic fin, and a black streak on upper jaw. Reaches at least 30 inches (76 cm). Indo-Pacific and tropical eastern Pacific, on coral reefs or rocky bottom.

CORNETFISHES (FISTULARIIDAE)

The cornetfishes are related to the trumpetfishes, and like them are very elongate with a long tubular snout, small oblique mouth, tiny teeth, and posterior position of the dorsal and anal fins. They differ notably in the body being depressed (broader than deep), by having a forked caudal fin with a long median filament, no fin spines, and short-based dorsal and anal fins. Cornetfishes also feed by sucking in their prey of small fishes in pipette fashion. They swim by undulation of the posterior part of the body. Four species are known, of which two occur in Hawai'i (one only in deep water).

CORNETFISH   nūnū peke   *Fistularia commersonii* Rüppell, 1838
Greenish dorsally, shading to silvery white below, with 2 blue stripes or rows of blue spots; a dark-barred pattern may be seen at night or when at rest near the bottom by day. Reported to 5 feet (150 cm), including the long caudal filament. Indo-Pacific and tropical eastern Pacific.

PIPEFISHES AND SEAHORSES (SYNGNATHIDAE)

Like the related trumpetfishes and cornetfishes, pipefishes and seahorses have a slender snout with a very small mouth at the end, feeding in the same pipette-like manner. These fishes are usually very slender, the body encased in bony rings; there is a very small gill opening, no spines in the fins, no pelvic fins, a single dorsal fin, and a very small anal fin (some species lack dorsal, anal, pectoral, and even the caudal fin). They usually feed on small free-living crustaceans such as copepods. The two pipefishes treated below sometimes clean other fishes. The reproduction is bizarre; the female deposits the eggs on the ventral surface of the male, usually in a pouch, and the "pregnant" male carries them until hatching. Pipefishes and seahorses are rarely seen because of their cryptic habits or camouflage. Eight species are reported from Hawaiian waters.

BLUESTRIPED PIPEFISH   *Doryrhamphus exisus* Kaup, 1856
Orange-yellow with a bluish lateral stripe, the broadly rounded caudal fin orange-yellow with orangish brown blotches and white upper and lower edges; trunk rings 17-19; tail rings 13-17. Maximum length, 2.7 inches (6.9 cm). Three subspecies: Red Sea, Indo-Pacific, and eastern Pacific. Usually seen in pairs.

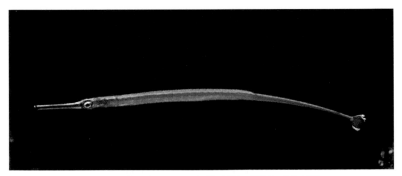

REDSTRIPE PIPEFISH   *Dunckerocampus baldwini* Herald & Randall, 1972
A red stripe on side of head and body (darker on snout); caudal fin red with white edges except posteriorly where blackish; body very elongate; snout long and slender, about 1.6 in head length. Attains 5.5 inches (14 cm). Hawaiian Islands; occurs in crevices and caves; known from 20-420 feet (6-128 m).

YELLOW SEAHORSE

Hippocampus kuda Bleeker, 1852

Color variable, but often yellow or yellow-ish brown; trunk rings 11; tail rings 34-37; spines or tubercles on head and ridges of body short; like other seahorses, tail prehensile and without a caudal fin. Reaches 12 inches (30 cm) outstretched. Indo-Pacific. Not common in Hawai'i and rarely seen; generally found in protected waters such as Kane'ohe Bay and Pearl Harbor. One record from a dredge haul in 180 feet (55 m). The thorny seahorse, *Hippocampus hystrix* Kaup, is recorded from a single poorly preserved specimen from Maui (verification of this record needed).

SCORPIONFISHES (SCORPAENIDAE)

The scorpionfishes are named for the venomous fin spines of many of the species. The most dangerous is the Stonefish (*Synancea verrucosa*) which has caused fatalities from wounds with its spines. Fortunately it does not occur in Hawai'i (although some people mistakenly call the larger Hawaiian species stonefishes). In Tahiti the stonefish is known as **nohu**. Not finding the stonefish in Hawai'i, early Tahitian immigrants applied the name to the larger Hawaiian scorpionfishes such as *Scorpaenopsis cacopsis*. Next in virulence of the spine venom are the turkeyfishes (*Pterois* spp.) and lionfishes (*Dendrochirus* spp.) of which there is one representative of each of

Leaf Scorpionfish

these genera in Hawaiian waters. If stuck by a venomous scorpionfish spine, place the wounded member in water as hot as can be tolerated; this will lessen the pain. Scorpionfishes have a reinforcing bony plate across the cheek below the eye, apparent as a ridge bearing small retrorse spines; there are other ridges and short spines on the head, including 3-5 spines on the preopercle and usually 2 on the opercle. Fishes of this family are well known for their camouflage; not only do they have mottled color patterns that match their surroundings, but many have fleshy flaps and small tentacles on the head and body. Most of these fishes are lie-and-wait predators that ambush small fishes and crustaceans that venture near. Many feed mainly at dusk or during the night. We are also fortunate in Hawai'i in not having any scorpionfishes of the Indo-Pacific subfamilies Choridactylinae (stingfishes) and Tetraroginae (waspfishes) which have virulently venomous spines.

HAWAIIAN LIONFISH *Dendrochirus barberi* (Steindachner, 1900)
Greenish to orangish brown with dark bars; eyes red; fins with rows of spots; tips of pectoral rays not free of membrane except lower rays; dorsal rays XIII,8-10, the spinous membranes incised nearly to back. Largest specimen, 6.5 inches (16.5 cm). Hawaiian Islands; usually beneath ledges or in recesses in reef; may occur as shallow as 3 feet (1 m) in calm areas. Wounds from spines extremely painful.

DECOY SCORPIONFISH *Iracundus signifer* Jordan & Evermann, 1903
Mottled red, usually with a small black spot between second and third dorsal spines; base of spinous portion of dorsal fin largely clear; fourth dorsal spine of adults notably longest; dorsal rays XII,9. Largest specimen, 5.1 inches (13 cm). Indo-Pacific. When undulated, the spinous dorsal fin resembles a small fish, the gap between the first and second spines seems like the mouth, the black spot the eye.

HAWAIIAN TURKEYFISH   nohu pinao   *Pterois sphex* Jordan & Evermann, 1903
Whitish to pink with dark brown bars; pectoral rays long, white, unbranched, and free of membrane for about half their length; dorsal rays XIII, 10, the spines long, deeply incised with little membrane, and very venomous. Largest, 8.3 inches (21 cm). Hawaiian Islands; usually concealed beneath ledges or in caves by day (often upside down). Take care putting your hands under ledges without looking first.

KELLOGG'S SCORPIONFISH   *Scorpaenodes kelloggi* (Jenkins, 1903)
Mottled brown and whitish with obscure bars; suborbital ridge usually with 3-4 spines; dorsal rays XIII,8; pectoral rays 18-19; longitudinal scale series about 30. Reaches 2 inches (5 cm). Indo-Pacific; not uncommon but rarely seen, due to both its camouflage and tendency to hide.

CHEEKSPOT SCORPIONFISH   *Scorpaenodes littoralis* (Tanaka, 1917)
Mottled brownish red with 4 squarish dark brown blotches along back below dorsal fin; a dark brown spot on operculum behind preopercle; dorsal rays XIII,9; pectoral rays usually 18-19; longitudinal scale series about 45. Attains 8 inches (20 cm). Indo-Pacific.

LOWFIN SCORPIONFISH *Scorpaenodes parvipinnis* (Garrett, 1864)
Color variable, often salmon pink with faint dark bars; sometimes a very broad white bar at front and middle of body; dorsal spines short, the longest less than eye diameter; dorsal rays XIII,9; pectoral rays 17-19; longitudinal scale series about 50. Reaches 5 inches (13 cm). Indo-Pacific, on reefs from the shallows to at least 160 feet (49 m).

SHORTSNOUT SCORPIONFISH *Scorpaenopsis brevifrons* Eschmeyer & Randall, 1975
Color highly variable; a blackish spot usually present near middle of spinous portion of dorsal fin; snout short with a steep profile; fourth to sixth dorsal spines longest; dorsal rays XII,9; pectoral rays 18-20; longitudinal scale series about 45. To 6 inches (15 cm). Indo-Pacific, but known from few localities.

TITAN SCORPIONFISH **nohu** *Scorpaenopsis cacopsis* Jenkins, 1901
Mottled orange-red; fleshy flaps on head and body well developed, especially on chin; third dorsal spine usually longest; dorsal rays XII,9; pectoral rays 17-19; longitudinal scale series 50-55. Attains 20 inches (51 cm). Hawaiian Islands; usually found in or near caves. A highly prized food fish, now difficult to find due primarily to impact on its population from spearfishing.

DEVIL SCORPIONFISH

nohu 'omakaha

Scorpaenopsis diabolus Cuvier, 1829

Color very variable, but inner surface of pectoral fins black in the axil, then yellow, and outwardly bright orange-red with a row of black spots; longitudinal scale series 43-48; a middorsal depression on top of head behind eyes and a deep one below front of eye. When alarmed, the pectorals are moved forward to reveal the bright inner colors (as warning coloration); a distinct hump on back centered below anterior spinous part of dorsal fin. Reaches about 12 inches (30 cm). Indo-Pacific, often on shallow reefs.

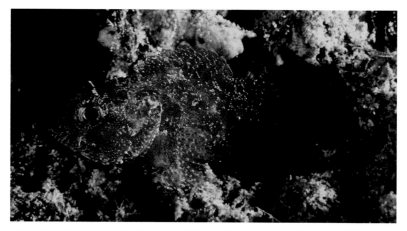

DWARF SCORPIONFISH   *Scorpaenopsis fowleri* (Pietschmann, 1934)
Red, mottled with white, usually with 2 dark bands radiating from rear half of eye; dorsal rays XII,9; pectoral rays 16; longitudinal scale series about 35. Currently in *Scorpaenopsis* due to lacking palatine teeth; may warrant placement in a new genus. Attains only 1.5 inches (4 cm). Hawai'i and French Polynesia to Maldive Islands, Indian Ocean.

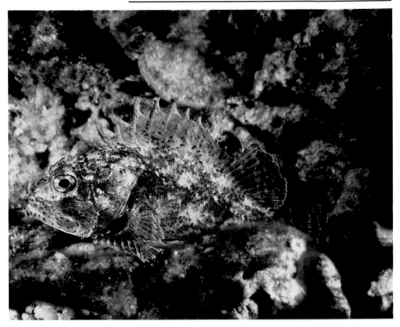

SPOTFIN SCORPIONFISH *Sebastapistes ballieui* (Sauvage, 1875)
Brown or greenish, mottled with white and spotted with dark brown or orange-red; often a large black-ish spot posteriorly in spinous part of dorsal fin; dorsal rays XII,9; pectoral rays 16; longitudinal scale series 40-45. Largest, 4.6 inches (11 cm). Hawaiian Islands.

SPECKLED SCORPIONFISH *Sebastapistes coniorta* Jenkins, 1903.
Speckled with numerous very small dark brown spots; no blackish spot in dorsal fin; dorsal rays XII,9; pectoral rays usually 16; longitudinal scale series 50-55; often with a tentacle-like cirrus above each eye. Largest, 3.8 inches (9.5 cm). Hawaiian Islands, Wake Island, and Line Islands; often shelters among branches of live coral. Occurs from near shore to at least 80 feet (24.5 m).

LEAF SCORPIONFISH   *Taenianotus triacanthus* Lacepède, 1802
May be black, red, yellow, brown, or nearly white, and variously blotched; body deep and compressed, the depth about 3 times the width. To 4 inches (10 cm). Indo-Pacific. Often rocks to and fro as if to simulate flotsam being moved by surge. It will do this even in an aquarium. Periodically sheds the outer layer of its skin. No reports of venomous fin spines.

HELMET GURNARDS (DACTYLOPTERIDAE)

The fishes of this small family are often called flying gurnards because they have very long pectoral fins which can be held to the side like those of flyingfishes. However, they are bottom-dwelling (except when larval), heavy, and slow-moving. They extend their pectoral fins laterally when alarmed, apparently to appear much larger to a potential predator. Helmet gurnards is a more appropriate name because the external bones of the head are united and armor-like, and the shoulder girdle on each side is expanded and shield-like posteriorly, ending in a sharp spine; also there is a long spine at the corner of the preopercle. The dorsal fin has 1 or 2 isolated anterior spines, the first just behind the head. These fishes live on open substrata of sand, rubble, or mud; the pelvic fins of I,4 rays are used for "walking" along the bottom. The most anterior pectoral rays are partly free of membrane and may be used to scrape into the sand to aid in the search for the usual food of crustaceans and small mollusks.

HELMET GURNARD   loloa'u   *Dactyloptena orientalis* (Cuvier, 1829)
Light greenish with dark brown spots dorsally, shading to white below; pectoral fins also dark-spotted except distally where irregularly lined with bright blue, the free ray tips white; pectoral fins reaching beyond caudal-fin base. Reported to 15 inches (38 cm). Indo-Pacific; usually on sand.

ORBICULAR VELVETFISHES (CARACANTHIDAE)

This family consists of a single genus, *Caracanthus*, and 4 small species, of which only one (formerly misidentified as *C. maculatus* occurs in Hawaiian waters (an old record of *C. unipinna* appears to be erroneous). These fishes are deep-bodied and compressed; there is a strong preorbital spine above the end of the upper jaw; the skin is covered with papillae; dorsal fin with VI-VIII spines and 11-14 rays; pelvic fins tiny, with I,2 or I,3 rays.

HAWAIIAN ORBICULAR VELVETFISH   *Caracanthus typicus* Krøyer, 1845.
Light gray with numerous small orange-red spots on head and body, shading to white ventrally; dorsal rays VIII,12, the fin deeply notched between spinous and soft portions; 5 broad spines on edge of preopercle. Reaches about 1.7 inches (4 cm). Hawaiian Islands; lives among branches of live coral.

GROUPERS, BASSLETS, AND ANTHIAS (SERRANIDAE)

The Serranidae is divided into five subfamilies of which three have species in the Hawaiian Islands: the Epinephelinae (groupers), Anthiinae (anthias), and Grammistinae (the Hawaiian representatives, three basslets of the genus *Liopropoma*). Compared to elsewhere in the Indo-Pacific region, the family is not well represented in Hawai'i. Only two native groupers occur in the islands, the giant *Epinephelus lanceolatus* (exceedingly rare; never seen by the author while diving in Hawai'i) and *E. quernus*, a deep-dwelling species. A third grouper, *Cephalopholis argus*, has been introduced from the Society Islands. Serranid fishes have a large mouth with the lower jaw projecting, the maxilla (posterior of two upper jaw bones) not part of the gape, its posterior end fully exposed on the cheek when mouth closed; there are 3 opercular spines. All of these fishes are carnivorous, the species of Epinephelinae feeding mainly on fishes and crustaceans and those of the Anthiinae on zooplankton, generally in aggregations. The fishes of these subfamilies are protogynous hermaphrodites, meaning that they commence mature life as females and change sex later to males.

PEACOCK GROUPER   **roi**   *Cephalopholis argus* Bloch & Schneider, 1801
Dark brown or olive-brown with numerous dark-edged bright blue spots; often with pale bars posteriorly on body and a pale area on chest; dorsal rays IX,15-17. Reaches 2 feet (60 cm). Indo-Pacific; introduced to the Hawaiian Islands from Moorea in 1956 (and with it, its Tahitian name **roi**). Most common at the island of Hawai'i. Large individuals have caused ciguatera fish poisoning in Hawai'i.

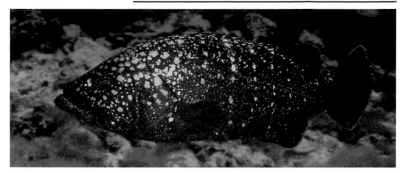

HAWAIIAN GROUPER   hāpu'u   *Epinephelus quernus* Seale, 1901
Adults dark brown with pale blotches and spots; juveniles dark brown with 8 vertical rows of small white spots on body; dorsal rays XI,14-15. Attains at least 32 inches (81 cm). Hawaiian Islands; adults in the main islands in deep water (the young occasional in diving depths); adults as shallow as 26 feet (8 m) in the Northwestern Hawaiian Islands.

YELLOW ANTHIAS   *Holanthias fuscipinnis* (Jenkins, 1901)
Orange-yellow with magenta markings; dorsal rays X,17, the third spine clearly longest; caudal fin forked. Reaches 9.5 inches (24 cm). Hawaiian Islands, generally at depths greater than 180 feet (55 m). Does well in aquaria despite its preference for deep water.

SUNRISE BASSLET *Liopropoma aurora* (Jordan & Evermann, 1903)
Red with small greenish to brownish yellow spots on body, yellow stripes and spots on head, and yellow bands in median fins; head pointed; dorsal rays VIII,13. Largest, 7.3 inches (18.5 cm). Hawaiian Islands, usually in 200 to least 600 feet (61-183 m); once observed by author in 120 feet (36.5 m)

EARLE'S SPLITFIN   *Luzonichthys earlei* Randall, 1981
Orange-yellow dorsally, abruptly magenta below; body slender; dorsal rays X - 16, the fin separated into spinous and soft portions; lateral-line scales 59-68. Attains 2.2 inches (5.6 cm). Hawai'i to Maldives; occurs to depths of at least 673 feet (205 m). When abundant, schools may be seen in 50 feet (15 m) or less.

BICOLOR ANTHIAS   *Pseudanthias bicolor* (Randall, 1979)
Yellow-orange on upper half of body, lavender to magenta on lower half; dorsal rays X,17-18, the third spine prolonged in females, the second and third very long in males, the expanded tips bright yellow; pectoral rays 19-21; lateral-line scales 54-64. Reaches 5 inches (13 cm). Hawai'i and New Caledonia to western Indian Ocean, usually at depths of 60-230 feet (18-70 m).

Male ⇑   ⇓ Female

HAWAIIAN LONGFIN ANTHIAS   *Pseudanthias hawaiiensis* Randall, 1979
Females yellow dorsally, shading to pale magenta below, with magenta lines around eye, and yellow
fins; head of males yellow, the body orange, flecked with magenta, becoming deep lavender posteriorly;
pelvic fins very long; dorsal rays X,17; pectoral rays 15; lateral-line scales 40-46. To 4 inches (10 cm).
Hawaiian Islands, usually in more than 100 feet (30.5 m). This fish was first described from Hawai'i by the
author as a subspecies, *Pseudanthias ventralis hawaiiensis*. The second subspecies *P. v. ventralis*, was
reported from other Pacific localities. Additional specimens have made the differences (larger size, higher
average number of gill rakers and different color in Hawai'i) more evident, so *hawaiiensis* is here
elevated to a species. *P. ventralis* is wide-ranging in the Pacific from Pitcairn Island to New Caledonia and
the Great Barrier Reef, north to southern Japan.

Male ⇑

⇓ Female

THOMPSON'S ANTHIAS   *Pseudanthias thompsoni* (Fowler, 1923)
Orange-red dorsally with a yellow spot on each scale; males with an oblique yellow-edged magenta band from snout across cheek, the lunate caudal fin magenta and yellow with a blue margin; posterior edge of orbit with papillae; dorsal rays X,16; pectoral rays 20-22; lateral-line scales 50-58. Males notably larger than females, the largest 8.5 inches (21.5 cm). This species was long believed to be restricted to the Hawaiian Islands, but in 1992 a specimen was collected by the author in the Ogasawara (Bonin) Islands, Japan at 140 feet (45 m). In Hawaii the species is known from the depth range of 16-523 feet (5-190 m). Feeds on zooplankton, mainly copepods and shrimp larvae. A fourth species of *Pseudanthias* is known from the Hawaiian Islands and Johnston Island, the colorful *P. fucinus* Randall and Ralston, distinct in its low lateral-line count of 34-36. It occurs from 550-775 feet (168-237 m).

FLAGTAILS (KUHLIIDAE)

Flagtails are silvery fishes with a moderately deep and compressed body, pointed head, and forked caudal fin usually marked with black; there are 2 spines on the opercle; the dorsal fin of X spines and 9-12 soft rays is deeply notched; there is a scaly sheath at the base of the dorsal and anal fins. The family consists of a single Indo-Pacific genus, *Kuhlia*, with about six species. One endemic species occurs in the Hawaiian Islands (Johnston Island has instead *K. marginata*). An attempt to introduce *K. rupestris* (Lacepède), a species usually found in brackish or freshwater, from Guam in 1958 was not successful. The listing of *K. taeniura* (Cuvier) = *K. mugil* (Forster & Schneider) from Hawaii by Tinker (1978) appears to be an error.

HAWAIIAN FLAGTAIL   āholehole   *Kuhlia sandvicensis* (Steindachner, 1876)
Silvery, the posterior edge of caudal fin blackish; dorsal rays X,11 or 12. Maximum length, 12 inches (30 cm). Hawaiian Islands; occurs near shore in marine, brackish, and freshwater habitats. Primarily nocturnal; feeds mainly on zooplankton, polychaete worms, insects, and algae. Usually seen in schools by day.

BIGEYES (PRIACANTHIDAE)

Priacanthid fishes are characterized by their very large eyes, moderately deep and compressed body, opercle with 2 flat spines, a serrate preopercle often with a broad spine at corner, highly oblique mouth with projecting lower jaw, and small rough scales. They are usually entirely red or dominantly red, but able to quickly change to silvery, blotched or barred with red, and even to entirely silvery. As their huge eyes would indicate, these fishes are nocturnal; they feed mainly on the larger animals of the zooplankton such as larval fishes, crustacean larvae, and larval polychaete worms. Four species occur in the Hawaiian Islands, two in deep water.

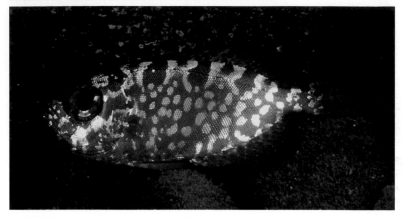

GLASSEYE   **'āweoweo**   *Heteropriacanthus cruentatus* (Lacepède, 1801)
Red, changing to silvery with numerous red blotches, to silvery pink; faint small dark spots on median fins, especially the caudal fin; a flat spine at corner of preopercle extending to edge of operculum. Largest recorded, 12.5 inches (32 cm). Circumtropical; usually found in less than 65 feet (20 m).

HAWAIIAN BIGEYE   **'āweoweo**   *Priacanthus meeki* Jenkins, 1903.
Red, but capable of changing to silvery pink; a row of small darker red blotches along lateral line; no spine at corner of preopercle of adults. Attains 13 inches (33 cm). Hawaiian Islands; closely related to *P. hamrur* Forsskål from elsewhere in the Indo-Pacific region.

HAWKFISHES (CIRRHITIDAE)

All of the fishes of this family have 14 pectoral-fin rays, the lower 5 to 7 of which are unbranched and thickened; there is a single dorsal fin of X spines and 11-17 rays which is notched between the spinous and soft portions; the tips of the dorsal spines have one or more projecting cirri. These fishes rest upon the reef, using their enlarged lower pectoral rays to wedge themselves in place if needed. All are carnivorous, typically darting out to prey upon small fishes and crustaceans. Some species, at least, are protogynous hermaphrodites (beginning mature life as females and changing sex later to males).

TWOSPOT HAWKFISH   **piliko'a**   *Amblycirrhitus bimacula* (Jenkins, 1903)
Whitish with large red blotches in vertical alignment; a pale-edged dark brown spot on opercle and another below rear base of dorsal fin; dorsal rays X,12; lower 5 pectoral rays unbranched. Largest, 3.3 inches (8.5 cm). Indo-Pacific; rarely seen in the open.

REDBARRED HAWKFISH   **piliko'a**   *Cirrhitops fasciatus* (Bennett, 1828)
White with 5 broad red bars on body, wider dorsally, and additional narrow red bars ventrally, one in each white interspace; a black spot on opercle; dorsal rays X,14; lower 6 pectoral rays unbranched. Reaches 4.5 inches (11.5 cm). Unusual disjunct distribution: Hawaiian Islands, Mauritius, and Madagascar.

STOCKY HAWKFISH   **po'opa'a**   *Cirrhitus pinnulatus* (Bloch & Schneider, 1801)
Body brownish gray with white blotches and small orange-red spots; body robust; dorsal rays X,11; lower 7 pectoral rays unbranched. Reported to 12 inches (30 cm). Indo-Pacific; lives in surge zone on reef or rocky bottom. Feeds mainly on crabs, but also other crustaceans, fishes, sea urchins, and brittle stars.

LONGNOSE HAWKFISH   *Oxycirrhites typus* Bleeker, 1857
Whitish with horizontal and near-vertical red bands forming a crosshatch pattern; snout long and pointed; dorsal rays X,13; lower 5 or 6 pectoral rays unbranched. Reaches 5.1 inches (13 cm). Indo-Pacific and tropical eastern Pacific; usually seen perched on black coral or gorgonians at depths greater than 100 feet (30.5 m). Feeds mainly on zooplankton. A popular aquarium fish.

White-Striped Phase ⇑   ⇓ Dark Brown Phase

ARC-EYE HAWKFISH   **piliko'a**   *Paracirrhites arcatus* (Cuvier, 1829)
Two color phases, one dark brown with darker brown stripes following scale rows, the other brownish red with a broad white to pink stripe on posterior two-thirds of body, both with a U-shaped mark of orange, black, and blue behind eye; dorsal rays X,11; lower 7 pectoral rays unbranched. To 5.5 inches (14 cm). Indo-Pacific; common in Hawai'i. The two color phases are not correlated with sex.

BLACKSIDE HAWKFISH **hilu piliko'a** *Paracirrhites forsteri* (Bloch & Schneider, 1801)
A broad black band on upper posterior half of body, ending in middle of caudal fin; head and anterior body with small dark red spots; dorsal rays X,11; lower 7 pectoral rays unbranched. Largest, 8.8 inches (22.5 cm). Indo-Pacific; feeds mainly on small fishes, occasionally on crustaceans.

MORWONGS (CHEILODACTYLIDAE)

The fishes of this small family are distinctive in the large number of dorsal spines and soft rays (XIV to XXII and 21 to 39). Also, like the hawkfishes, they have the lower pectoral rays unbranched and enlarged. They have a small mouth, small teeth, thick lips, and a forked caudal fin. The species occur in warm temperate to subtropical seas (none from the tropics). The postlarval stage is large. One taken from a tern's nest in Hawai'i was mistakenly described as a new genus and species, *Gregoryina gygis*, and placed in a new family *Gregoryinidae* by Fowler and Ball (1924).

HAWAIIAN MORWONG **kikākapu** *Cheilodactylus vittatus* Garrett, 1864.
Light olivaceous with 2 oblique black bands on body and 3 on head; adults with a pair of bony protuberances on forehead and a second pair at front of snout; fourth dorsal spine notably longest. Attains 16 inches (40 cm). Antitropical; Hawai'i in the north and New Caledonia and Lord Howe Island in the south. Feeds on a wide variety of very small invertebrates.

CARDINALFISHES (APOGONIDAE)

The cardinalfishes are named for the red color of some of the species. The family is characterized by having two dorsal fins, the first of VI to VIII spines, and the second of a single spine and 8-14 soft rays; an anal fin with II spines and 8-18 soft rays (II,8 in all Hawaiian species except the deep-water *Lachneratus phasmatodes*); large eyes; a large mouth; and a double-edged preopercle. Most species are small, generally less than 12 cm. They are nocturnal (though a few of the larger species may feed opportunistically by day). Most feed mainly on the larger animals of the plankton, but some prey primarily on small crustaceans on or near the bottom. Those for which the reproductive habits are known are mouth brooders. After fertilization of the ova, the male incubates them in his mouth until hatching. Ten species occur in the Hawaiian Islands; the six most often seen by divers are presented below.

HAWAIIAN RUBY CARDINALFISH   'upāpalu   *Apogon erythrinus* Snyder, 1904.
Translucent red (internal bones of body visible in life); dorsal rays VI - I,9 (other Hawaiian species with VII - I,9, except *A. evermanni*); pectoral rays 14-15. Reaches 2.3 inches (5.8 cm). Hawaiian Islands; closely related to *A. crassiceps* from elsewhere in the Pacific. A common inshore species, but generally seen only at night (and then close to shelter, to which it quickly moves if illuminated).

ODDSCALE CARDINALFISH   'upāpalu   *Apogon evermanni* Jordan & Snyder, 1904
Red with a black spot at rear base of second dorsal fin and a small white spot just behind it; a dark brown streak across head; dorsal rays VI - I,9; lateral-line scales 24; remaining scales of body small, 45-48 in longitudinal series; caudal peduncle long. Reaches 6 inches (15 cm). Indo-Pacific and tropical western Atlantic; occurs deep in caves, usually in more than 75 feet (23 m).

IRIDESCENT CARDINALFISH　'upāpalu　*Apogon kallopterus* Bleeker, 1856
Light brown (with blue-green iridescence at night), with a narrow dark brown stripe on head, continuing less marked on side of body and ending in a small dark spot at caudal-fin base (stripe and spot on body may be diffuse or absent in large adults); both borders of preopercle serrate. Attains 6 inches (15 cm); Indo-Pacific; often the most common cardinalfish of shallow reefs.

SPOTTED CARDINALFISH　'upāpalu　*Apogon maculiferus* Garrett, 1863
Pinkish to orangish gray with rows of small dark brown spots following series of scales of body, and a dusky spot at midbase of caudal fin; outer edge of preopercle serrate, the inner edge largely smooth. Reaches 5.5 inches (14 cm). Hawaiian Islands; more common at the northwestern end of the chain. Occurs from 3 to at least 100 feet (1-30.5 m).

BANDFIN CARDINALFISH　'upāpalu　*Apogon menesemus* Jenkins, 1903
Light brown with a pale-edged black band in all fins except pectorals, the one in each lobe of caudal fin usually linked by a dark bar near fin base; iridescent at night. Largest, 7.1 inches (18 cm). Hawaiian Islands; very closely related to *A. taeniopterus* from elsewhere in the Indo-Pacific (the latter without a dark bar in caudal-fin, and with 14 instead of 13 pectoral rays). This photograph was taken at night.

BAY CARDINALFISH **'upāpalu** *Foa brachygramma* (Jenkins, 1903)
Finely blotched light gray to yellowish brown with iridescence; outer part of anterior membranes of spinous dorsal fin white; both edges of preopercle smooth; caudal fin rounded (usually forked in *Apogon*). Largest, 3.1 inches (8 cm). Indo-Pacific; usually found around dead coral, sponges, or heavy plant growth in shallow bays or harbors. Common in Kane'ohe Bay, O'ahu.

TILEFISHES (MALACANTHIDAE)

The tilefishes (also known as blanquillos) have a single sharp opercular spine and long unnotched dorsal and anal fins, the dorsal with I-X spines, the anal with I or II. The tilefish family is divisible into two subfamilies, the sand tilefishes (Malacanthinae), represented in Hawaiian waters by a single species of *Malacanthus*, and the Latilinae (deep-water species, none in Hawai'i). Frequently seen in pairs.

FLAGTAIL TILEFISH **maka 'ā** *Malacanthus brevirostris* Guichenot, 1848
Light gray, shading to white on side, often with faint gray bars; 2 black stripes in middle of caudal fin; body very elongate. Attains 12 inches (30 cm). Indo-Pacific and tropical eastern Pacific; usually found in sand or rubble-sand areas; builds a burrow, often under a surface rock, in which it seeks refuge when approached; a pile of rubble may be present near burrow entrance.

REMORAS (ECHENEIDAE)

The remoras, also called sharksuckers or diskfishes, have a broad flat head bearing a unique, transversely ridged, oval, sucking disk with which they are able to attach to other marine animals. These fishes have an elongate body and long spineless dorsal and anal fins which are elevated anteriorly. Most remoras are associated with one or a few host species; the two species of *Echeneis* are not host-specific and are free-living part of the time. *E. naucrates* is the species most often encountered inshore in Hawai'i. *Remora remora* may be found on large sharks such as the tiger shark, and *Remorina albescens* on mantas.

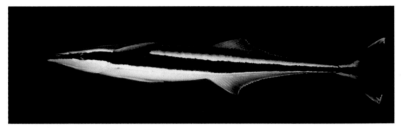

SHARKSUCKER   **leleiona**   *Echeneis naucrates*   Linnaeus, 1758
Gray with a white-edged lateral black stripe from tip of lower jaw to base of caudal fin; body very elongate; disk laminae 21-28. Reported to 3 feet (91 cm). Circumglobal in tropical to warm temperate seas; attaches to sea turtles and a wide variety of fishes, often on sharks.

JACKS (CARANGIDAE)

The jacks are a large family of strong-swimming, open-water, carnivorous fishes which are usually silvery in color. Although not reef fishes in the sense of residing on coral reefs, they often prey upon reef fishes or feed on zooplankton near reefs; they also may come to cleaning stations in reefs. Jacks vary greatly in shape from fusiform, such as the species of *Decapterus*, to deep-bodied, as seen in the species of *Alectis* and *Caranx*. The caudal peduncle is slender and usually reinforced by a series of external overlapping bony plates called scutes; the caudal fin is strongly forked to lunate. The eye is generally protected by the transparent so-called adipose eyelid (but immovable and not fatty). There are 2 separate dorsal fins, the first of IV to VIII spines (first dorsal fin embedded in adults of a few species); the anal fin nearly always has 2 initial spines which are detached from the rest of the fin. The family is well represented in Hawai'i with 24 species.

The general Hawaiian name for the species of jacks and trevallies (*Carangoides* and *Caranx*) is **ulua**; the young are called **pāpio**. The larger jacks and trevallies are highly prized gamefishes.

AFRICAN POMPANO   **ulua kihikihi**

Alectis ciliaris (Bloch, 1788)

Silvery blue dorsally, silvery below with iridescence; a black blotch at base of third to sixth dorsal soft rays; juveniles with 5 slightly chevron-shaped dark bars; dorsal rays VII + 1,18-20; however the spines of the first dorsal fin are embedded with growth; anal rays II + 15-17, the spines are also embedded in adults; anterior 4 or 5 dorsal and anal rays extremely elongate in juveniles (believed to be mimicking venomous jellyfishes such as cubomedusae). Reaches at least 50 inches (127 cm); world angling record, 50.5 lbs (22.9 kg). Circumtropical. Also known as threadfin jack. Adults called **kagami ulua** in Hawai'i, a hybrid Japanese/Hawaiian name. *Carangoides ajax* Snyder, described from Hawai'i, is a synonym based on the adult form. The record of *Alectis indicus* (Rüppell) from the Hawaiian Islands is an error.

⇑ Juvenile

BARRED JACK   ulua   *Carangoides ferdau* (Forsskål, 1775)
Silvery blue-green dorsally, shading to silvery on side and ventrally, with 7 gray bars on upper two-thirds of body nearly as broad as pale interspaces. Largest, 21 inches (53 cm). Indo-Pacific; rare in Hawai'i. Often seen in small schools; feeds mainly on benthic crustaceans, occasionally on small fishes.

ISLAND JACK   ulua   *Carangoides orthogrammus* (Jordan & Gilbert, 1882)
Silvery blue-green on back, shading below to silvery, usually with several small elliptical yellow spots
with dusky centers on side of body. Largest, 27.5 inches (70 cm). Indo-Pacific and tropical eastern Pacific.
Feeds on benthic crustaceans, worms, and small fishes, mainly on sand bottoms.

GIANT TREVALLY   ulua aukea   *Caranx ignobilis* (Forsskål, 1775)
Silvery gray, shading ventrally to silvery white, with numerous very small black spots; centers of scutes
blackish; mature males may be nearly black; dorsal soft rays 18-21. Reaches at least 65 inches (165 cm);
world angling record, 145 lbs (66 kg), from Maui. Indo-Pacific; common in the Northwestern Hawaiian
Islands. Often occurs in small schools; feeds mainly on fishes.

BLACK TREVALLY   ulua lā'uli   *Caranx lugubris* Poey, 1860
Dark olive-gray to almost black dorsally, shading to bluish gray ventrally, the scutes black; dorsal profile
of snout to above eye straight to slightly concave; dorsal soft rays 20-22. Attains 32 inches (81 cm). Circumtropical; usually seen on outer reef slopes at depths greater than 100 feet (30.5 m).

BLUEFIN TREVALLY   'ōmilu   *Caranx melampygus* Cuvier, 1833
Brassy dorsally, shading to silvery with iridescence below, finely blotched with bright blue and dotted with small black spots; fins blue; dorsal soft rays 21-24. Reported to 39 inches (100 cm); world angling record, 96 lbs (43.5 kg). Indo-Pacific and tropical eastern Pacific; the most common of the larger jacks in Hawai'i. Feeds primarily on fishes. The young may be found in small schools, sometimes in estuaries.

BIGEYE TREVALLY   pake ulua   *Caranx sexfasciatus* Quoy & Gaimard, 1824
Silvery gray dorsally, grading to silvery white ventrally, the scutes black; a small black spot on operculum at upper end of gill opening; tips of second dorsal and anal fins white; eye large; dorsal soft rays 19-22. Reaches 33 inches (85 cm). Indo-Pacific and tropical eastern Pacific. Nocturnal; forms dense schools by day. Sometimes seen in courtship pairs at dusk, the presumed male nearly black.

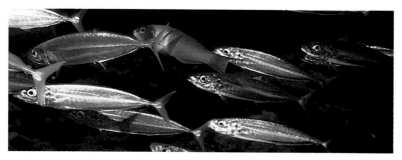

MACKEREL SCAD   'ōpelu   *Decapterus macarellus* Cuvier, 1833
Silvery blue-green on back, silvery on side and ventrally, with a small black spot at edge of operculum at level of eye; caudal fin yellowish; body elongate and only slightly compressed; last dorsal and anal rays as a separate finlet. Reported to 12.5 inches (32 cm). Circumtropical; a schooling species known from near the surface to over 650 feet (200 m); feeds on zooplankton. Most common of 4 species in Hawai'i.

RAINBOW RUNNER   **kamanu**   *Elagatis bipinnulata* (Quoy & Gaimard, 1824)
Olive green on back; side of body with a yellow stripe edged in bright blue; ventral part of body white; body elongate; no scutes. Reaches 4 feet (120 cm); world angling record 37 lbs, 9 oz (17 kg). Circumtropical; often occurs in small schools. Feeds mainly on small fishes and the larger crustaceans of the zooplankton. Highly esteemed as a food fish, and highly prized as a game fish.

GOLDEN TREVALLY

ulua pa'opa'o

Gnathanodon speciosus

(Forsskål, 1775)

Juveniles golden yellow with narrow black bars; adults silvery with iridescence and a few scattered blackish blotches, the dark bars faint or absent; lips very fleshy; juveniles with a

⇑ **Juvenile**

few feeble teeth in the lower jaw (the generic name *Gnathanodon* is from the Greek meaning toothless jaws; the specific name *speciosus* is Latin for beautiful); adults without teeth; adipose eyelid poorly developed .Reaches a length of 4 feet (120 cm). Indo-Pacific and tropical eastern Pacific from Baja California to Peru. Usually seen over sandy bottoms; feeds on sand-dwelling invertebrates and small fishes. The young sometimes ride the bow wave of large fishes.

THICKLIPPED JACK   butaguchi, buta ulua   *Pseudocaranx dentex* (Bloch & Schneider, 1801)
Iridescent silvery with a narrow brassy stripe (more evident in young than adults); a black spot on opercle at level of eye; snout pointed, the dorsal profile slightly concave; lips thick and fleshy. Reported to 37 inches (94 cm). Circumglobal in subtropical and warm temperate seas; common in the Northwestern Hawaiian Islands. Rare and in deep water in the main islands.

LEATHERBACK   lai   *Scomberoides lysan* (Forsskål, 1775)
Silvery with 2 longitudinal series of small blackish spots on body; outer half of anterior lobe of soft dorsal fin black; body moderately elongate and strongly compressed; scales slender and pointed; posterior dorsal and anal rays joined only basally by membrane. Reaches 27 inches (68 cm). Indo-Pacific; may occur as solitary individuals or in small groups. *Chorinemus sanctipetri* Cuvier is a synonym.

BIGEYE SCAD   akule   *Selar crumenophthalmus* (Bloch, 1793)
Silvery blue-green dorsally, shading to iridescent silvery below, usually with a brassy stripe on side of body; a blackish spot at edge of opercle; no finlets. Attains 11 inches (28 cm). Worldwide in tropical and subtropical seas. Forms small to large schools from near shore to depths as great as 560 feet (170 m); feeds primarily on zooplankton. Sometimes classified in the genus *Trachurops*.

GREATER AMBERJACK kāhala *Seriola dumerili* (Risso, 1810)
Silvery blue-gray to olive gray on back, silvery white ventrally, with a midlateral yellow stripe and an oblique olive-brown band from mouth through eye to nape; no scutes. Reported to 74 inches (188 cm); world angling record, 155 lb, 10 oz (70.6 kg). Circumtropical; occurs from near shore to more than 1200 feet (366 m); worst offender for causing ciguatera in Hawai'i.

SNAPPERS (LUTJANIDAE)

The snappers are small to moderate in size with an ovate to somewhat elongate body; the mouth is fairly large; the upper part of the maxilla (posterior bone of upper jaw) slips under the preorbital bone when the mouth is closed; the dorsal fin is continuous, often notched, with X-XII (usually X) dorsal spines and 9-17 soft rays; the anal fin has III spines and 7-11 soft rays. All of the species are carnivorous, and many are nocturnal. They are among the most important commercial fishes of tropical and subtropical seas. Hawai'i has only two native shallow-water species, *Aphareus furca* and *Aprion virescens*; however, three species of  *Lutjanus* have been introduced from French Polynesia. One of these, the small Bluestripe Snapper (*L. kasmira*) has become extremely abundant in Hawaiian waters; fishermen believe it has caused a diminution in the populations of some native fishes of greater value than itself; also it is suspected of depleting the population of kona crabs. Of special importance as food fishes in Hawai'i are the deeper water snappers *Aphareus rutilans*, two species of *Etelis*, and four species of *Pristipomoides*.

SMALLTOOTH JOBFISH   wahanui   *Aphareus furca* (Lacepède, 1802)
Silvery lavender-brown on back, shading to silvery gray on side; edges of opercle and preopercle black-ish; occasional individuals with a patch of yellow dorsally on head; mouth large but teeth very small; caudal fin deeply forked. Attains about 15 inches (38 cm). Indo-Pacific; a free-swimming predaceous species that ranges over reefs in quest of its usual prey of small fishes.

GREEN JOBFISH   uku   *Aprion virescens* Valenciennes, 1830.
Greenish gray dorsally, shading to silvery gray ventrally; a series of blackish spots, one per membrane, basally on posterior spinous portion of dorsal fin; body elongate; strong canine teeth anteriorly in jaws; caudal fin deeply forked. Attains nearly 40 inches (100 cm). Indo-Pacific and tropical eastern Pacific; a roving open-water predator of reef fishes; occasionally takes crustaceans and octopus. Difficult to approach. One eaten by the author in Mauritius gave him ciguatera fish poisoning.

BLACKTAIL SNAPPER   to'au   *Lutjanus fulvus* (Forster & Schneider, 1801).
Yellowish; caudal fin black with a tinge of red and a narrow white posterior margin; dorsal fin dark or-ange-red, the remaining fins yellow; caudal fin slightly emarginate. Reaches 13 inches (33 cm). Indo-Pacific; introduced to Hawai'i from Moorea in 1956 but not common; usually solitary. Feeds principally on crabs and small fishes. The young may be found in brackish water.

BLUESTRIPE SNAPPER　ta'ape　*Lutjanus kasmira* (Forsskål, 1775)
Yellow with 4 narrow dark-edged bright blue stripes on head and body; caudal fin slightly forked. Largest, 15 inches (38 cm); rarely exceeds 12 inches (30 cm). Indo-Pacific; introduced to Hawai'i from the Marquesas in 1958. Forms large semi-stationary schools by day; disperses to feed at night, mainly on crustaceans and small fishes. Occurs from the shallows to 900 feet (275 m).

EMPERORS (LETHRINIDAE)

The fishes of this family are related to the snappers. They have an unnotched dorsal fin with X spines and 9 or 10 soft rays, and an anal fin of III spines and 8-10 soft rays; the caudal fin is forked. All of the emperors have strong canine teeth at the front of the jaws, but the teeth vary on the side of the jaws, depending on the species, from conical to molariform.

There are five genera, *Lethrinus* with 28 species, *Gymnocranius* with eight species, and *Gnathodentex*, *Monotaxis*, and *Wattsia*, with one each. The only Hawaiian representative of the family is the **mu**, *Monotaxis grandoculis*. All except one species occur in the Indo-Pacific region. The species of *Lethrinus* include some with long pointed snouts; the best known and largest is *L. olivaceus* which reaches a length of 40 inches (1 m). All of the teeth of this species are pointed. It is primarily a fish-feeder, and the one most often implicated in ciguatera fish poisoning. The species with nodular to molariform teeth on the side of the jaws tend to feed on hard-shelled invertebrates such as mollusks and sea urchins. Twelve juveniles of an unknown species of *Lethrinus* from the Marquesas were among the fishes released into Kane'ohe Bay, O'ahu in 1958 at the time the bluestripe snapper, *Lutjanus kasmira*, was introduced. Perhaps fortunately, the *Lethrinus* did not become established.

BIGEYE EMPEROR   mu

Monotaxis grandoculis (Forsskål, 1775)

Olive to gray-brown dorsally, silvery on side and ventrally; able to rapidly assume a pattern of 4 very broad blackish bars on about upper third of body (persistent black bars in juveniles); eye very large; snout blunt in adults, pointed in young; side of jaws with well-developed molars. Attains nearly 2 feet (60 cm). Indo-Pacific. Nocturnal; feeds mainly on mollusks, hermit crabs, sea urchins, and heart urchins. The hard parts of the prey are crushed by the molar teeth; most of the hard fragments are ejected. Adults are difficult to approach underwater, especially during the day.

⇑ **Juvenile**

THREADFINS (POLYNEMIDAE)

This family of fishes consists of seven genera and 33 species. The most distinctive feature of the family is the structure of the pectoral fins; they are low on the body and divided into an upper part with the rays joined by membrane, and a lower part of 3 to 7 separate filamentous rays. The common name Threadfins is derived from these slender separate rays. The number of these rays is often helpful for identifying species, and for some it was the basis of the scientific name. For example, the one Hawaiian species of the family, *Polydactylus sexfilis*, has six separate pectoral rays (*sexfilis*, from the Latin, means six threads). Polynemid fishes are also distinctive in having an overhanging obtusely conical snout, an adipose eyelid (firm transparent tissue covering eye), two widely separated dorsal fins (the first of VII or VIII spines), and a large forked to lunate caudal fin. They are shallow-water fishes that live on sand or mud bottoms. When searching for food, their separate lower pectoral rays are held forward to contact the bottom (hence similar to the use of the pair of chin barbels by goatfishes). Their food consists primarily of shrimps, crabs, polychaete worms, and other invertebrates.

SIX-FINGERED THREADFIN   **moi**   *Polydactylus sexfilis* (Valenciennes, 1831)
Silvery white with dark lines following scale rows; pectoral fins dark gray, the separate lower rays white; pectoral rays 15 + 6 (as free thread-like rays); caudal fin large and deeply forked. Reaches about 18 inches (46 cm). Oceanic islands from Hawai'i and French Polynesia to Seychelles and Mauritius; occurs along sandy shores, often in small schools. Excellent eating. In ancient Hawai'i, **moi** were reserved for chiefs. On the island of Hawai'i, the Hawaiians had four names for the different growth stages.

MULLETS (MUGILIDAE)

Mullets have moderately elongate bodies that are little-compressed except posteriorly; the head tends to be depressed, the interorbital space broad. The mouth is small, terminal to slightly inferior, and usually shaped like an inverted V when viewed from the front; there is a fleshy median knob in the upper lip of most species; the teeth are absent or minute and set in the lips. The intestine is very long; most mullets have a gizzard-like stomach. There are 2 well separated dorsal fins, the first of IV spines. There is no distinct lateral line, but most scales of the body have a longitudinal groove. Typically, mullets feed on fine algal and detrital material from either hard substratum or the surface of bottom sediments, retaining the food within their numerous fine gill rakers and expelling inorganic sediment from the gill openings. Some ingest algal scums from the surface. Mullets are often seen in small schools. They are prone to leap free of the surface (hence may be difficult to catch in a seine). Two native species occur in Hawaiian waters. A third, the small *Moolgarda engeli*, was unintentionally introduced to Hawai'i in 1955 with a shipment of Marquesan sardines from Nuku Hiva.

The Striped Mullet, **'ama'ama** *(Mugil cephalus),* was very important to the ancient Hawaiians; they had different names for the growth stages. Small juveniles (**pua'ama'ama**) were caught with nets along sandy shores and reared in ponds built with rock walls in shallow areas where there is freshwater drainage. This is still done in some areas today.

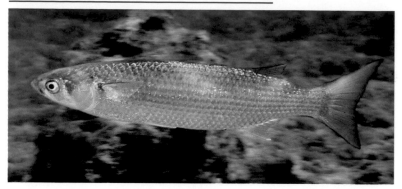

STRIPED MULLET   **'ama'ama**   *Mugil cephalus* Linnaeus, 1758.
Silvery gray dorsally, silvery on sides, with faint gray-brown stripes following centers of scale rows; edge of caudal fin usually blackish; snout blunt; transparent adipose eyelid covering front and back of eye; anal rays III,8. Reports of lengths to 3 feet (29cm) seem exaggerated; any fish over 20 inches (50 cm) are unusual. Circumglobal in subtropical to warm temperate seas; the possibility of different species or subspecies over this vast range warrants investigation.

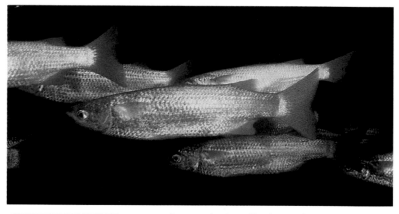

SHARPNOSE MULLET   **uouoa**   *Neomyxus leuciscus* (Günther, 1871)
Silvery greenish gray dorsally, silvery on side and below, with a small yellow spot at upper base of pectoral fins; body slender; snout pointed; no adipose eyelid; anal rays III,10. Rarely exceeds 12 inches (30 cm). Islands of Oceania. Occurs in small schools close to shore, over both rocky bottom and sand.

GOATFISHES (MULLIDAE)

Goatfishes are readily identified by a pair of long barbels at the front of the chin; they have a moderately elongate body and 2 well-separated dorsal fins, the first of VIII (rarely VII) spines and 9 soft rays; all have I,7 anal rays. These fishes use their barbels, which possess chemosen-

sory organs, to probe into the bottom in search of food organisms. When prey are located in sand or mud, the goatfishes root into the sediment with their snouts. They feed mainly on worms, crustaceans, brittle stars, small mollusks, and heart urchins; a few species feed in part on small fishes. Males rapidly wriggle their barbels during courtship. Ten native species are known from Hawaiian waters, and one, *Upeneus vittatus*, was unintentionally introduced from the Marquesas; it inhabits mud bottoms.

YELLOWSTRIPE GOATFISH   **weke 'ā**   *Mulloidichthys flavolineatus* (Lacepède, 1801)
Greenish gray, shading to silvery white below, with a yellow stripe on side; a blackish spot usually present in stripe below first dorsal fin; fins whitish; body elongate. Reaches 16 inches (40 cm). Indo-Pacific. Usually encountered by day in aggregations that remain in the same general area. These disperse at night when most feeding takes place. The young of this species and other **weke** are called **'oama**.

PFLUGER'S GOATFISH   **weke nono**   *Mulloidichthys pflugeri* (Steindachner, 1900)
Reddish gray, shading to pale gray ventrally, the fins reddish; when foraging, 4 broad red bars on body (as shown in the photograph), the last centered on caudal-fin base; most of the head red; peritoneum white (dark brown on other species of the genus). Largest, 19 inches (50 cm). Indo-Pacific, mainly from oceanic islands. Usually found at depths greater than 75 feet (23 m).

YELLOWFIN GOATFISH **weke 'ula** *Mulloidichthys vanicolensis* (Valenciennes, 1831).
Yellowish gray dorsally, silvery white to pink below, with a yellow lateral stripe; fins yellow. Attains 15
inches (38 cm). Indo-Pacific; tends to occur in deeper water than *M. flavolineatus*. Forms semi-stationary
schools over reefs by day; forages individually at night over sand substrata.

DOUBLEBAR GOATFISH **munu** *Parupeneus bifasciatus* (Lacepède, 1801)
Yellowish gray to reddish with 2 broad dark bars on body and a third fainter bar often present on caudal
peduncle; barbels short; snout short, its dorsal profile slightly concave. Attains 13 inches (33 cm). Indo-
Pacific. Feeds on crabs, shrimps, other crustaceans, octopuses, small fishes, and polychaete worms.

YELLOWBARBEL GOATFISH   *Parupeneus chrysonemus* (Jordan & Evermann, 1903)
Whitish with 2 brownish red stripes, one along back (containing dark brown flecks) and one from snout,
through eye, and along upper side; barbels yellow (or partly red) and long. Reaches 9 inches (23 cm).
Hawaiian Islands; in deep water off main islands, but in diving depths in Northwestern Hawaiian Islands.

BLUE GOATFISH   moano kea   *Parupeneus cyclostomus* (Lacepède, 1801)
Yellowish gray with blue markings on scales, blue lines from eyes, and a large yellow saddle-like spot on
caudal peduncle; barbels very long (as long as head); snout long. To 20 inches (50 cm). Indo-Pacific. Unusual in feeding heavily on fishes (about 70% of the diet); uses its barbels to probe into holes to frighten
out small fishes. A common color phase away from Hawai'i is bright yellow.

MANYBAR GOATFISH   moano   *Parupeneus multifasciatus* (Quoy & Gaimard, 1824)
Whitish to light red or light bluish brown with 3 or 4 dark bars on posterior half of body, the broadest
below second dorsal fin; a dark stripe behind eye; barbels fairly long; last dorsal and anal rays distinctly
longer than penultimate rays. Largest, 11.3 inches (29 cm). Central and western Pacific; most common
species of the genus in Hawaiian waters. Feeds mainly on crustaceans.

SIDESPOT GOATFISH **malu** *Parupeneus pleurostigma* (Bennett, 1830)
Whitish to pink with blue spots on head and back and a large black spot on upper side below rear of first dorsal fin, followed by a large diffuse white spot; base of second dorsal fin blackish; barbels fairly long; last dorsal and anal rays longer than penultimate rays. Attains 13 inches (33 cm). Indo-Pacific.

WHITESADDLE GOATFISH **kūmū** *Parupeneus porphyreus* (Jenkins, 1903)
Olivaceous to red with a saddle-like white spot anteriorly on caudal peduncle and 2 oblique whitish bands dorsally on head and anterior body; barbels fairly short; pectoral rays usually 15 (most often 16 in other Hawaiian species of the genus). Reported to 16 inches (41 cm). Hawaiian Islands; occurs from inshore to 460 feet (140 m). Closely related to *P. ischyrus* (Snyder) of Japan.

BANDTAIL GOATFISH **weke pueo** *Upeneus arge* Jordan & Evermann, 1903
Silvery with 2 orange-yellow stripes on side of body and black cross bands in each lobe of the deeply forked caudal fin (5-6 in lower lobe of adults); body elongate. Attains about 12 inches (30 cm). Indo-Pacific; usually found in small groups on sand bottoms near shallow reefs. The introduced *U. vittatus* has 3 or 4 black bands on the lower caudal lobe.

SEA CHUBS (KYPHOSIDAE)

The sea chubs, also called rudderfishes, are shore fishes of rocky bottoms or coral reefs of exposed coasts. They have relatively deep oval bodies, a continuous dorsal fin, usually with XI spines, and a forked caudal fin; the mouth is small with close-set incisiform teeth, well adapted to feeding on their usual food of benthic algae; the digestive tract is very long. The species of *Kyphosus* often occur in aggregations; when feeding as a group, they are able to overwhelm the defenses of territorial damselfishes and surgeonfishes. There are four species of the family in Hawai'i, three in the drab genus *Kyphosus* and the colorful semipelagic *Sectator ocyurus* (olivaceous yellow with 2 bright blue stripes). *S. ocyurus* is rare in Hawai'i and may only be a waif from the tropical eastern Pacific.

GRAY CHUB   **nenue**   *Kyphosus bigibbus* Lacepède, 1801
Gray to gray-brown dorsally, the scale centers silvery; side of body with faint narrow bronze stripes following scale rows; opercular membrane blackish; soft portion of dorsal fin not higher than longest spines. Dorsal rays usually XI,12; anal rays III,11. Indo-Pacific. To 2 feet (60 cm). All-yellow fish sometimes seen, and rarely white ones; crosses of these with normal-colored individuals are known.

HIGHFIN CHUB   **nenue**   *Kyphosus cinerascens* (Forsskål, 1775)
Gray-brown, the centers of scales usually paler than edges; soft portion of dorsal fin distinctly higher than longest dorsal spine; dorsal rays usually XI,12; anal rays III,11; a slight convexity in dorsal profile of head in front of upper part of eye. Reported to 20 inches (51 cm). Indo-Pacific; less common than the other two species of *Kyphosus* in Hawai'i, and less apt to form aggregations.

LOWFIN CHUB **nenue** *Kyphosus vaigiensis* (Quoy & Gaimard, 1825)
Very similar in color to the Gray Chub, but the stripes on the body and cheek are more distinct and more brassy; soft portion of dorsal fin not higher than longest dorsal spines; dorsal rays usually XI, 14; anal rays III, 13. Reaches 2 feet (60 cm). Indo-Pacific; may occur as solitary fish or in schools. Feeds mainly on algae, like others of the genus.

STRIPIES (MICROCANTHIDAE)

This family of three small genera is sometimes regarded as a subfamily of the Kyphosidae, but stripies differ in having slender pointed teeth in many rows rather than a single row of incisiform teeth. They are often placed in the halfmoon family Scorpididae, and in the older literature they were classified as butterflyfishes (Chaetodontidae) because of their deep bodies, small mouths, brush-like teeth, and distinct color patterns. However, they seem best treated as a separate family. Only one species occurs in Hawai'i.

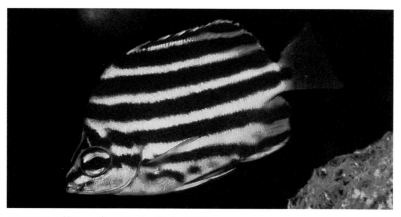

STRIPEY *Microcanthus strigatus* (Cuvier, 1831)
Yellow to whitish with 6 oblique black stripes which are narrower ventrally; body deep and compressed; snout short but pointed; dorsal rays XI, 16 or 17; caudal fin slightly emarginate. Largest, 7.7 inches (19.5 cm). Antitropical; occurs in Hawai'i, Japan, China, Australia, and New Caledonia, generally in turbid lagoons, bays, or harbors. Omnivorous; does well in an aquarium.

BUTTERFLYFISHES (CHAETODONTIDAE)

These colorful fishes are high-bodied, ovate, and strongly compressed with small mouths and a band of brush-like teeth in the jaws; there is no spine on the cheek at the corner of the preopercle (as seen in the angelfishes); the dorsal fin is continuous or slightly notched, with VI-XVI strong spines and 15-30 soft rays, the anterior interspinous membranes deeply incised; the caudal fin varies from slightly rounded to slightly emarginate. Many of the species feed on polyps of corals or on other coelenterates (those that are obligate coral-polyp feeders should not be collected for aquaria). Other butterflyfishes feed heavily on benthic algae and small bottom-dwelling invertebrates such as polychaete worms and crustaceans. Some such as the species of *Hemitaurichthys* are primarily zooplankton-feeders. Most butterflyfishes are solitary or occur in pairs; a few such as *Heniochus diphreutes* form aggregations. Those oriented to the bottom tend to form territories; some have relatively small territories while others wander over a large area of reef. Many of the species have a black bar on the head which encloses the eye. Butterflyfishes are diurnal; they take cover in the reef at night, generally exhibiting a different color pattern from that of the day. The family is well represented in Hawaiian waters by 24 species (two of these occur in deep water, and *Chaetodon ulietensis* is known from only two specimens, hence appears to be a waif). Two general Hawaiian names, **kikākapu** and **lauhau**, are applied to all but a few of the chaetodontids, as might be expected from their limited value as food fishes.

THREADFIN BUTTERFLYFISH   kikākapu   *Chaetodon auriga* Forsskål, 1775
White with 2 series of diagonal dark lines at right angles, shading posteriorly to orange-yellow; black bar on head broad below eye; a black spot in outer soft portion of dorsal fin; dorsal rays XIII,23-25, the fourth to sixth soft rays prolonged as a filament. To 8 inches (20 cm). Indo-Pacific. Feeds principally on worms, coelenterates, and algae.

SPECKLED BUTTERFLYFISH   lauhau   *Chaetodon citrinellus* Cuvier, 1831
Pale yellow with a small bluish spot on each body scale; a black bar through the eye and a broad black margin on anal fin; dorsal rays usually XIV,20-22. Attains 5 inches (13 cm). Indo-Pacific; rare in Hawai'i. Feeds on algae, coral polyps, and other small invertebrates. Also known as the Citron Butterflyfish.

SADDLEBACK BUTTERFLYFISH   kikākapu   *Chaetodon ephippium* Cuvier, 1831
Gray with a large black area, rimmed anteriorly in white, on dorsoposterior part of body and extending broadly into dorsal fin; blue stripes on lower side of body; ventral part of head and chest orange-yellow; dorsal rays usually XIII,23-25, the fourth to sixth soft rays of adults prolonged as a filament. To 9 inches (23 cm). Central and western Pacific; not common in Hawai'i.

BLUESTRIPE BUTTERFLYFISH   **kikākapu**   *Chaetodon fremblii* Bennett, 1829
Yellow with narrow oblique bright blue bands, a black spot on nape, and a larger one posteriorly on body
which extends into rear of dorsal fin; dorsal rays XIV,20-22. Reaches 6 inches (15 cm). Known only from
Hawaiian Islands; a common species in shallow water, but has been reported to 600 feet (183 m). Feeds
on tentacles of tubeworms, a variety of other invertebrates, and algae.

BLACKLIP BUTTERFLYFISH   **lauhau**   *Chaetodon kleinii* Bloch, 1790
Body yellow with a bluish spot on each scale and a broad diffuse brown bar anteriorly; a blue or bluish
brown bar from nape to eye, continuing as black through eye and below; lips blackish; dorsal rays usually
XIII,21-22. Reaches 5 inches (13 cm). Indo-Pacific, generally below 40 feet (12 m). Feeds mainly on zooplankton and soft corals. Also known as Klein's Butterflyfish.

LINED BUTTERFLYFISH   **kikākapu**   *Chaetodon lineolatus* Cuvier, 1831
White with vertical black lines on body; a broad black arc posteriorly on body, enclosing a median white spot on the forehead; median fins yellow; dorsal rays XII,24-27. Largest butterflyfish; reaches 12 inches (30 cm). Indo-Pacific; generally inshore, but submarine observations to 560 feet (171 m). Feeds mainly on coral polyps and anemones. Closely related to the large *C. oxycephalus* of the Indo-Malayan region.

RACCOON BUTTERFLYFISH   **kikākapu**   *Chaetodon lunula* (Lacepède, 1802)
Body dusky dorsally, shading to orange-yellow below, with oblique reddish stripes and 3 broad yellow-edged black bands; head with a broad black ocular bar, followed by a wide white one; dorsal rays XII,23-24. Reaches 8 inches (20 cm). Indo-Pacific. Mistakenly reported as nocturnal; feeds on a wide variety of invertebrates and sometimes on algae. May occur in aggregations.

OVAL BUTTERFLYFISH **kapuhili** *Chaetodon lunulatus* Quoy & Gaimard, 1825
Orange-yellow with narrow, slightly diagonal, purplish stripes; front of snout black, separated from black ocular bar by orange-yellow; dorsal rays XIII,21-22. To 5.5 inches (14 cm). Central and western Pacific; occurs on reefs in calm lagoons and bays; feeds on coral polyps. Nearly always encountered in pairs. Very similar to *C. trifasciatus* of the Indian Ocean which has an orange bar at the base of the caudal fin.

MILLETSEED BUTTERFLYFISH

lau wiliwili

Chaetodon miliaris Quoy & Gaimard, 1825

Bright yellow with vertical rows of small black-ish spots; a black ocular bar, and a broad black bar across caudal peduncle; dorsal rays XIII,21-23. Attains 6.5 inches (16.5 cm). Hawaiian Islands where it is the most common species of the family; occurs from the shallows to 820 feet (250 m). Feeds mainly on zooplankton; sometimes cleans other fishes. Also called the Lemon Butterflyfish.

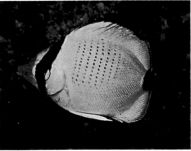

⇑ Juvenile

MULTIBAND BUTTERFLYFISH   kikākapu   *Chaetodon multicinctus* Garrett, 1863
White with narrow brown bars and speckled with small olive-brown spots (darker within brown bars);
black ocular bar interrupted on forehead; caudal peduncle with a narrow black bar; dorsal rays XIII,24-26.
Attains 4.7 inches (12 cm). Hawaiian Islands; occurs in pairs. Feeds principally on coral polyps.

ORNATE BUTTERFLYFISH   kikākapu   *Chaetodon ornatissimus* Cuvier, 1831
Body white with 6 oblique orange bands; head yellow with 5 black bars, one of which extends into dorsal
fin for its entire length; dorsal rays XII,25-27. Reaches 8 inches (20 cm). Central and western Pacific; also
Christmas Island in the eastern Indian Ocean, and one record from Sri Lanka. Feeds on coral polyps; therefore should not be considered for aquaria. Occurs in pairs.

FOURSPOT BUTTERFLYFISH   lauhau   *Chaetodon quadrimaculatus* Gray, 1831
Upper half of body dark brown with 2 white spots, lower half orange-yellow with a small brown spot on each scale; ocular bar orange, narrowly edged in black and blue; a narrow dark-edged blue band in dorsal and anal fins. Attains 6 inches (15 cm). Islands of Oceania, mainly in outer reef areas. Feeds primarily on coral polyps. Frequently seen in pairs.

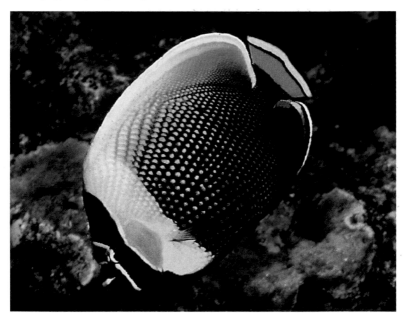

RETICULATED BUTTERFLYFISH   *Chaetodon reticulatus* Cuvier, 1831
A broad yellow-edged black bar on head through eye, followed by a very broad light gray zone to pectoral region; rest of body black with a pale yellow spot on each scale; dorsal rays XII,27-28. Reaches 7 inches (18 cm). Central and western Pacific, usually seen in pairs in outer reef areas. Not common; most often seen at the island of Hawai'i. Feeds on coral polyps, occasionally on algae.

TINKER'S BUTTERFLYFISH   *Chaetodon tinkeri* Schultz, 1951
Head white with an orange-yellow ocular bar; body white with small black spots to a demarcation from base of fourth dorsal spine through middle of anal fin, then black; caudal fin yellow; dorsal rays XIII, 20-22; soft portion of dorsal fin lower than spinous. To 7 inches (18 cm). Hawai'i and Marshall Islands; rare in less than 100 feet (30.5 m). Diet varied; does well in aquaria.

CHEVRON BUTTERFLYFISH   *Chaetodon trifascialis* Quoy & Gaimard, 1825
Body white with narrow chevron-shaped markings; head white with black ocular bar; caudal fin largely black; less deep-bodied than other chaetodontids; dorsal rays XIII-XIV, 14-16. Attains 7 inches (18 cm). Indo-Pacific; usually found on *Acropora* coral on which it feeds. Very rare in Hawai'i; occurs at French Frigate Shoals where *Acropora* is reported. Common at Johnston Island. Maintains a small territory with vigor. Perhaps the most pugnacious of butterflyfishes.

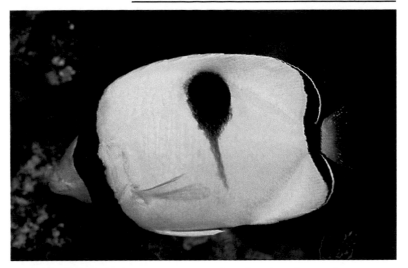

TEARDROP BUTTERFLYFISH   kikākapu *Chaetodon unimaculatus* Bloch, 1787
Body yellow dorsally, shading to white below, with a large black spot on upper side that narrows ventrally to a blackish line; ocular black bar broad; jaws heavier than other chaetodontids. Largest 7.8 inches (20 cm). Indo-Pacific (but yellow in Indian Ocean). Often bites into the hard septa when feeding on corals; also eats worms, crustaceans, and algae. Usually encountered in pairs.

FORCEPSFISH   lau wiliwili nukunuku 'oi'oi *Forcipiger flavissimus* Jordan & McGregor, 1898
Body, dorsal, anal, and pelvic fins yellow; nape and upper half of head black, lower half and chest white; snout extremely long and slender, more than half head length; a distinct cleft to mouth. To 7.2 inches (18.5 cm). Indo-Pacific and tropical eastern Pacific. Feeds on worms, small crustaceans, tubefeet and pedicellariae of sea urchins, and fish eggs.

LONGNOSE BUTTERFLYFISH

lau wiliwili nukunuku 'oi'oi

Forcipiger longirostris Broussonet, 1782

Two color phases, one dark brown, the other nearly the same as the preceding species, but chest has rows of blackish dots; snout even longer than that of the Forcepsfish, and cleft of mouth very short. Largest, 8.6 inches (22 cm). Indo-Pacific. Feeds mainly on small crustaceans.

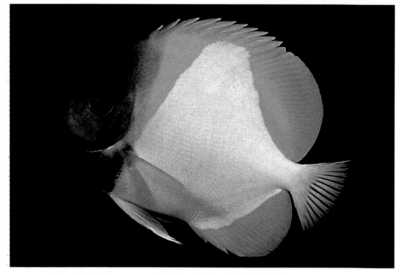

PYRAMID BUTTERFLYFISH   *Hemitaurichthys polylepis* (Bleeker, 1857)
Head and body anterior to base of third dorsal spine brown, followed by a triangular yellow zone (broader at top) continuous with dorsal fin; most of body white (narrow dorsally due to yellow below soft portion of dorsal fin); outer part of anal fin yellow. Reaches 7 inches (18 cm). Central and western Pacific. Feeds on zooplankton, often in aggregations, on outer reef slopes. Sometimes called the Brownface Butterflyfish.

THOMPSON'S BUTTERFLYFISH   *Hemitaurichthys thompsoni* Fowler, 1923
Gray-brown without conspicuous markings; snout short but protruding; lateral-line complete (ending below rear of dorsal fin in *Chaetodon*), the scales small (76-87 in lateral line).Largest, 8.4 inches (21 cm). Islands of the Pacific Plate; usually from outer reef areas at depths greater than 33 feet (10 m); one from 980 feet (300 m). Feeds on zooplankton; often seen in small aggregations.

PENNANTFISH   *Heniochus diphreutes* Jordan, 1903
White with 2 broad oblique black bands on body; soft dorsal, caudal, and pectoral fins yellow; fourth dorsal spine and membrane extremely prolonged as a white filament; dorsal rays XII,23-25. Reaches 8 inches (20 cm). Indo-Pacific, mainly in subtropical localities. Feeds on zooplankton, often in schools; also cleans other fishes. The look-alike non-Hawaiian *H. acuminatus* usually has XI,25-27 dorsal rays.

ANGELFISHES (POMACANTHIDAE)

Once classified as a subfamily of the butterflyfishes, the angelfishes are now known to be a distinct family. They share many of the characters of the chaetodontids, such as the deep compressed body, small mouth with brushlike teeth, small scales which extend well out onto the median fins, and a single unnotched dorsal fin. They differ most obviously in having a strong spine on the cheek at the corner of the preopercle. Their larval development is also very different. Angelfishes are diurnal. Many of the large species, such as those of the genus *Pomacanthus,* feed heavily on sponges, whereas small species such as those of the genus *Centropyge* feed on benthic algae and detritus. Because of the beautiful colors of most of the angelfishes, they are popular aquarium fishes. Some (perhaps all) of the angelfishes are protogynous hermaphrodites, i.e. they begin mature life as females and change later to males, with some change in color pattern in some species. One individual of the gaudily colored Emperor Angelfish (*Pomacanthus imperator*) was caught off Kona in 1948 (hence probably not an aquarium release), and there have been two other sightings since then. These were probably only stragglers that drifted in as larvae from distant shores, not representatives of a breeding population in the islands. *Centropyge nahackyi* was described recently from specimens taken in deep-diving depths at Johnston Island and one from Kona, Hawaii.

FISHER'S ANGELFISH *Centropyge fisheri* (Snyder, 1904)
Orange, overlaid with brown in broad central region of body; a large bluish black spot above pectoral-fin base; caudal and pectoral fins yellowish; edge of pelvic and anal fins blue. Reaches 3 inches (7.5 cm). Hawaiian Islands, generally in more than 50 feet (15 m). Like others of the genus, stays close to shelter. *C. flavicauda* from elsewhere in the Indo-Pacific is a close relative, if not conspecific.

JAPANESE ANGELFISH   *Centropyge interrupta* (Tanaka, 1918)
Orange on head and most of body with small irregular bright blue spots, shading to dark blue or brown on lower posterior part of body and to yellow on caudal peduncle and fin; edge of dorsal, anal, and pelvic fins bright blue. Reported to 6.3 inches (16 cm). Known only from Japan, Taiwan, and the Northwestern Hawaiian Islands. Not reported from Hawai'i until 1981.

FLAME ANGELFISH   *Centropyge loricula* (Günther, 1873)
Bright red with 3-7 black bars on side of body, the first broader and shorter (occasional bars double or branched); dorsal and anal fins banded posteriorly with purple-blue and black (more evident in males). Largest, 3.9 inches (10 cm). Islands of Oceania; rare in Hawaiian waters. A highly prized aquarium fish.

POTTER'S ANGELFISH   *Centropyge potteri* (Jordan & Metz, 1912)
Head, upper anterior part of body, chest, and abdomen with alternating irregular lines of orange and grayish blue; side and posterior part of body with irregular vertical lines of blue and black. Attains 5 inches (12.7 cm). Hawaiian Islands; the most common of Hawaiian angelfishes and among the most common of reef fishes in the islands. Important in the aquarium fish trade

BANDIT ANGELFISH   *Desmoholacanthus arcuatus* (Gray, 1831)
A broad white-edged black band from snout through eye to posterior part of dorsal fin; back above band brown with a small white spot on each scale; body below band pale gray with small white spots; a broad white-edge black band in caudal and anal fins. To 7 inches (18 cm). Hawaiian Islands; usually seen at depths of more than 100 feet (30.5 m). Feeds mainly on sponges.

Male ⇑   ⇓ Female

MASKED ANGELFISH   *Genicanthus personatus* Randall, 1975
Females white with a black area on front of head, usually enclosing eye, and a broad back bar on basal three-fifths of caudal fin; males (a result of sex reversal) white with head anterior to edge of preopercle orange-yellow, and all but basal part of dorsal and anal fins bright orange. Attains about 10 inches (25 cm). Hawaiian Islands; rare in the main islands except in deep water, but not uncommon in the North-western Hawaiian Islands below depths of about 90 feet (27.5 m). Feeds principally on zooplankton.

ARMORHEADS (PENTACEROTIDAE)

The fishes of this family are known as boarfishes in Australia. They are distinctive in having the head encased in exposed striated bones; the body is compressed and moderately to very deep; the dorsal fin is continuous with IV-XV strong spines. Most of the species occur in deep water. Of the two which are found in the Hawaiian Islands, only one is apt to be seen by divers.

WHISKERED ARMORHEAD   *Evistias aculirostris* (Temminck & Schlegel, 1844)
Body white to yellow with 5 broad black bars; protruding snout deep blue; fins except pelvics mainly yellow; dorsal rays IV-V,26-28, the last spine longest; numerous short whisker-like barbels on chin. Attains 2 feet (60 cm). Known from Hawai'i, Japan, Lord Howe Island, Kermadec Islands, and North Island, New Zealand (hence antitropical in distribution). Usually found at depths greater than 60 feet (18 m) Nocturnal. One brought to the Waikiki Aquarium would not accept any food and it gradually wasted away. Fecal pellets of a second fish revealed that it had eaten brittlestars. It was then successfully fed brittlestars, and later adapted to other food.

KNIFEJAWS (OPLEGNATHIDAE)

This family of a single genus derives its common name from its jaws, the teeth of which are coalesced into a sharp parrot-like beak. These fishes are moderately deep-bodied and compressed; the dorsal fin is long-based with XI or XII spines; anterior part of soft portions of the dorsal and anal fins elevated. Scales small, ctenoid, and adherent. Knifejaws are reported as omnivorous, but they feed more on animal material than plant. With their strong, sharp jaws they can easily crush mollusks and barnacles. Young knifejaws are found at the surface with drifting seaweed. At a length of about 2 inches (5 cm), they move to the bottom. Initially they have separate incisiform teeth, but with growth these coalesce into a beak. The family is antitropical in distribution, with three species in South Africa, one in southern Australia, two in Japan and Hawai'i, and one from the Galapagos Islands south to Chile. The two species in Japan are esteemed as food fishes; they have been artificially propagated. Hybrids of these two species have been reported.

BARRED KNIFEJAW *Oplegnathus fasciatus* (Temminck & Schlegel, 1844)
Light gray-brown with 5 dark brown bars on body (bars more distinct in juveniles and may be absent in large adults); dorsal rays XI-XII,17-18. Attains 31.5 inches (80 cm). Japan and Hawai'i; rare in the main islands, but occasional inshore in the Northwestern Hawaiian Islands.

SPOTTED KNIFEJAW *Oplegnathus punctatus* (Temminck & Schlegel, 1844)
Light gray with small irregular black spots, more evident on head, chest and median fins (black spots relatively larger and more distinct on juveniles); front of snout and chin white in large adults; dorsal rays XII,15-16. Reported to 34 inches (86 cm). Japan, Marianas, and Hawai'i; rare in the main islands, but not uncommon in the Northwestern Hawaiian Islands.

DAMSELFISHES (POMACENTRIDAE)

Damselfishes (or demoiselles) are among the most abundant of reef fishes. They are small, moderately deep-bodied, with a small mouth and conical or incisiform teeth. There is a continuous dorsal fin of X-XIV spines, the base of the spinous portion longer than the soft, and II anal spines; the caudal fin varies from truncate to lunate (but usually forked). The lateral-line is interrupted, the anterior part ending below the dorsal fin. The coloration is highly variable from species to species; some are drab, others brilliantly hued. The juveniles of many are very different in color and more brightly colored than adults. Males generally show a different color pattern

at spawning time. Most damselfishes occur in shallow water
on coral reefs or rocky substrata.
Many, particularly those that
feed heavily on benthic algae,
such as the species of *Stegastes*,
are territorial and pugnacious
(hence not good aquarium
fishes). The algal feeders are
known to "weed" their territories of undesirable algae. The
species of *Chromis* and *Dascyllus* feed primarily on zooplank-

Male Hawaiian Sergeant guarding its nest.

ton, often in small aggregations. *Plectroglyphidodon johnstonianus*
is among the few that feed on coral polyps. The eggs of damselfishes
are elliptical and demersal; the male parent guards the patch of eggs
until hatching. If the guarding male is frightened away, as by a diver,
other fishes (usually wrasses and butterflyfishes) quickly seize the
opportunity to feed on the eggs. Seventeen species of pomacentrid
fishes are known from Hawai'i. Not included below are the deep-
water *Chromis struhsakeri* and the inshore pink-barred
Plectroglyphidodon phoenixensis, recorded only from one small
colony at Maui. The latter lives in the surge zone of exposed rocky
shores.

HAWAIIAN SERGEANT   **mamo**   *Abudefduf abdominalis* (Quoy & Gaimard, 1825)
Light blue-green, shading through pale yellow on side to white ventrally, with 5 blackish bars on body
that become narrow and faint ventrally; juveniles yellow with black bars; dorsal rays XIII,13-15. Largest,
9.8 inches (25 cm). Hawaiian Islands. Abundant; occurs inshore in calm bays, in deeper water on exposed
coasts. Feeds mainly on zooplankton, but algae are also eaten.

BLACKSPOT SERGEANT **kūpīpī** *Abudefduf sordidus* (Forsskål, 1775)
Yellowish gray with 7 broad dark brown bars on body, the upper end of sixth bar (at front of caudal peduncle) with a large black spot; dorsal rays XIII, 14-16 (usually 15). Largest, 9.3 inches (23.5 cm). Indo-Pacific. Lives inshore on rocky bottom, often where surge is strong; young common in tidepools. Feeds on algae, crabs and other crustaceans, sponges, polychaete worms, etc.

INDO-PACIFIC SERGEANT **mamo** *Abudefduf vaigiensis* (Quoy & Gaimard, 1825)
Light blue-green with 5 black bars on body about as broad as pale interspaces; often bright yellow dorsally on body; dorsal rays XIII, 12-14. Reaches 8 inches (20 cm). Indo-Pacific; appears to be a recent immigrant to Hawai'i; small breeding colonies have been observed at the islet of Molokini and on O'ahu. Very closely related to the Sergeant Major (*A. saxatilis*) of the western Atlantic.

DWARF CHROMIS   *Chromis acares* Randall & Swerdloff, 1973
Blue-gray with a small light yellow spot at rear base of dorsal fin; front half of anal fin black except for blue leading edge; upper and lower edges of caudal fin broadly yellow; dorsal rays XII,11. Attains 2.2 inches (5.5 cm). Central and western Pacific; rare in Hawai'i, but common at Johnston Island.

AGILE CHROMIS   *Chromis agilis* Smith, 1960
Orange-brown, suffused with lavender or pink over lower head and chest; caudal fin whitish; a large black spot at base of pectoral fins; dorsal rays XII,12-14. Largest, 4.4 inches (11 cm). Indo-Pacific; appears to be more common on lee side of islands; known from the depth range of 15 to at least 200 feet (4.5-61 m). Like others of the genus, feeds on zooplankton.

CHOCOLATE-DIP CHROMIS   *Chromis hanui* Randall & Swerdloff, 1973
Dark yellowish brown, the caudal peduncle and fin abruptly white slightly posterior to rear base of dorsal and anal fins; no pink or lavender on lower head and chest, but snout and jaws often tinged with blue; a large black spot at base of pectoral fins; dorsal rays XII,13. Attains 3.5 inches (9 cm). Hawaiian Islands; known from the depth range of 6-165 feet (1.8-50 m).

WHITETAIL CHROMIS *Chromis leucura* Gilbert, 1905
Dark brown to bluish gray, abruptly white on posterior half of caudal peduncle, caudal fin, and posterior part of dorsal and anal fins; a large black spot at base of pectoral fins, usually followed by a yellow bar; pelvic fins largely yellow; dorsal rays XII,14. Attains 2.5 inches (6.5 cm). Indo-Pacific; found usually at depths below about 80 feet (24.5 m).

Juvenile ⇓   Adult ⇑   ⇓ Subadult

OVAL CHROMIS *Chromis ovalis* (Steindachner, 1900)
Yellowish green, the scale edges narrowly blackish; lips pink; upper base and axil of pectoral fins black; small juveniles bright blue, the dorsal fin and a band along back yellow; larger juveniles yellow with a blue streak extending behind upper part of eye; dorsal rays XIV,11-13. Reaches 7.5 inches (19 cm). Hawaiian Islands; abundant. Forms zooplankton-feeding aggregations.

BLACKFIN CHROMIS   *Chromis vanderbilti* (Fowler, 1941)

Greenish gray dorsally, shading to yellow, with blue spots forming stripes along scale rows; lower edge of caudal fin broadly black; anal fin bluish black except for last few rays and blue leading edge; dorsal rays XII,11. Hawaiian Islands and Pitcairn Island to the western Pacific. A coral-reef species usually seen in less than 60 feet (18.3). Occurs in aggregations. It is surprising that such a widespread, common, shallow-water damselfish was not described and named until 1941.

THREESPOT CHROMIS

Chromis verater Jordan & Metz, 1912

Dark brown to nearly black with 3 white spots, one at rear base of dorsal fin, one at rear base of anal fin, and one at mid-base of caudal fin (white spots sometimes faint); dorsal rays XIV,12-14. The largest of the genus in Hawai'i; reaches 8.5 inches (21.5 cm). Hawaiian Islands; usually found at depths greater than 60 feet (18.3 m); abundant below 200 feet (61 m), and known to at least 600 feet (183 m). Feeds on a wide variety of zooplankton, especially copepods (70% of the diet).

⇧ **Juvenile**

HAWAIIAN DASCYLLUS   'alo'ilo'i

Dascyllus albisella Gill, 1862

Dark gray to nearly black, centers of scales on body broadly white to bluish white; small juveniles blacker with a vertically elongate white spot on side and median blue spot on forehead; body deep. To 5 inches (12.5 cm). Hawaiian Islands; young usually hide among branching corals in quiet shallow water; adults range into deeper water. Close to the Indo-Pacific *D. trimaculatus*. Feeds on the small animals of the zooplankton such as mysids, crab and shrimp larvae, and copepods. Spawns mainly May to August; eggs demersal, almost colorless, and tiny (0.85 mm); newly transformed juveniles average 0.6 inches (15 mm).

⇑ **Juvenile**

BRIGHTEYE DAMSELFISH   *Plectroglyphidodon imparipennis* (Vaillant & Sauvage, 1875)
Yellowish gray, shading to white ventrally and light yellow posteriorly; eye white with a black bar through pupil; dorsal rays XII, 14-16. Attains 2.5 inches (6.5 cm). Indo-Pacific; occurs inshore on exposed reefs or rocky bottom; quick to take shelter in small holes. Feeds on a variety of small invertebrates, especially crustaceans and polychaete worms.

BLUE-EYE DAMSELFISH   *Plectroglyphidodon johnstonianus* Fowler & Ball, 1924
Yellowish gray; a large elliptical blackish bar usually present posteriorly on body and extending into soft part of dorsal and anal fins; blue markings on head; iris blue; dorsal rays usually XII, 18. Lips fleshy and vertically furrowed. Largest, 4.7 inches (12 cm). Indo-Pacific. Closely associated with live coral, especially branching *Pocillopora*; feeds in part on coral polyps, for which its fleshy lips appear to be an adaptation.

ROCK DAMSELFISH   *Plectroglyphidodon sindonis* (Jordan & Evermann, 1903)
Dark brown, the edges of scales darker than centers, with 2 well-separated narrow whitish bars in middle of body; juveniles with a large pale-edged black spot on back and base of soft dorsal fin; dorsal rays XII, 19-20. Reaches 5 inches (12.5 cm). Hawaiian Islands; inhabits surge zone of exposed rocky shores. Feeds mainly on algae, occasionally on small invertebrates.

PACIFIC GREGORY

Stegastes fasciolatus (Ogilby, 1889)

Brownish gray, often with indistinct dark blotches, the edges of scales dark brown (giving an effect of dark vertical lines); iris yellow; juveniles with yellow caudal peduncle and fin, the dorsal fin with a bright blue margin and large black spot near the front. Attains 6.3 inches (16 cm). Indo-Pacific; common in Hawai'i. Feeds mainly on benthic algae and detritus.

⇑ Juvenile

WRASSES (LABRIDAE)

The wrasses are a large and diverse family, varying greatly in size and shape. Typically they have thick lips, protruding front canine teeth, and nodular to molariform teeth in the pharyngeal region. The scales are cycloid (smooth-edged); the head is scaleless or with just the cheek and opercle scaled. There is a single unnotched dorsal fin of VIII-XXI spines, and the anal fin usually has III spines. Most wrasses are brightly and complexly colored. Juveniles frequently have a very different color pattern from adults.

Sex reversal from female to male has been demonstrated for many wrasses and may be true of all species of the family. The change in sex is generally accompanied by a change in color pattern; the resulting terminal male is usually more vividly colored. Some terminal males, as well as juveniles, are so different in color that they were often named as different species.

Many species, such as those of the genera *Stethojulis* and *Thalassoma,* have identically colored mature males and females in the first color phase (termed the initial phase). These spawn in aggregations dominated by males. The release of eggs and sperm takes place at the peak of a rapid upward rush from the aggregation. Terminal males establish sexual territories and spawn individually with females in their harem. Wrasses are diurnal; at night most of the smaller species bury in the sand to sleep; the larger ones hide deep within the reef. All wrasses are carnivorous; most, such as the species of *Bodianus*, *Coris*, and *Thalassoma*, feed on a variety of hard-shelled invertebrates such as crabs, hermit crabs, mollusks, sea urchins, and brittle stars which they crush with their powerful pharyngeal dentition. Some of the larger wrasses such as *Coris gaimard* and *Novaculichthys taeniourus* turn over rocks to expose the invertebrates hiding beneath. The species of *Anampses* strike the bottom forcefully with their projecting teeth, sucking in very small animals such as crustaceans, Foraminifera, and mollusks, along with sand and debris; the species of *Stethojulis* do the same, but are more inclined to pick up sand. A few wrasses feed mainly on fishes; some such as the species of *Cirrhilabrus* are zooplankton-feeders; a few with very fleshy lips feed on coral polyps; and some such as those of the genus *Labroides* are cleaners or part-time cleaners (meaning they remove skin parasites and some mucus of other fishes).

Wrasses swim mainly with their pectoral fins, bringing their tails into action only when swift movement is needed. Most are closely associated with coral reefs or rocky substrata, but the razorfishes (*Xyrichtys* spp.) and knifefishes (*Cymolutes* spp.) live over open sand bottom. With their compressed bodies and thin foreheads, they are able to dive into sand to escape predation. The Labridae is represented in Hawai'i by 43 species, more than any other shore fish family; some occur only at depths greater than penetrated by divers. The general Hawaiian name for most wrasses is **hinālea**; the small species usually have no specific Hawaiian name. The wrasses *Thalassoma lutescens* and *T. quinquevittatum* are rare in Hawaiian waters. They occasionally hybridize with *T. duperrey* (documentation will be provided by Phillip S. Lobel and the author).

The hybrid *Thalassoma duperrey* X *Thalassoma lutescens*, Johnston Island.

Male ⇑   ⇓Female

PSYCHEDELIC WRASSE   *Anampses chrysocephalus* Randall, 1958
Body of males brown with a blue spot on each scale, the head bright orange with blue markings, the caudal fin with a cream-colored bar at base; females brown with a white spot on each scale, the caudal fin red with a broad white bar toward the base. Attains 7 inches (18 cm). Hawaiian Islands. Usually seen at depths greater than 50 feet (15 m); juveniles and females often swim in small groups.

Pearl Wrasse (Male)   See description on the next page.

PEARL WRASSE **'opule** *Anampses cuvier* Quoy & Gaimard, 1824 ⇑ **Female**
Body of males yellowish to greenish with a vertical blue line on each scale and a faint pale bar in pectoral region; upper anterior part of head green, the rest with a reticulum of blue lines; females brown, shading to red below, with a white spot on each scale; chest and lower head white with small red spots. Reaches about 14 inches (35.5 cm). Hawaiian Islands; primarily an inshore species of rocky bottom.

Hawaiian Hogfish (Male). See description on the next page.

Hawaiian Hogfish (Female). See description on the next page.

HAWAIIAN HOGFISH 'a'awa

Bodianus bilunulatus (Lacepède, 1801)

Males blotchy dark reddish to purplish brown; females white with brown lines that become yellow posteriorly; a large oblong black spot below rear of dorsal fin; caudal, anal, and posterior dorsal fin yellow; juveniles yellow dorsally, black posteriorly, with a white caudal fin. Largest, 20 inches (51 cm). Indo-Pacific; the Hawaiian population recognized as a subspecies, *Bodianus bilunulatus albotaeniatus* (Valenciennes).

⇑ Juvenile

SUNRISE WRASSE *Bodianus sanguineus* (Jordan & Evermann, 1903)
Bright red with a yellow stripe from front of snout along upper side; a broad yellow stripe on head below eye; a black spot on opercle and another at base of caudal fin; dorsal and caudal fins yellow. Reaches at least 7.5 inches (19 cm). Hawaiian Islands; a rare species known from few specimens, all from depths greater than 100 feet (30.5 m); submarine observations to 550 feet (168 m).

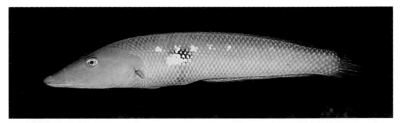

Male ⇑   ⇓ Female

CIGAR WRASSE **kupoupou** *Cheilio inermis* (Forsskål, 1775)
Olive green, brown, orange-brown, or yellow, often with a narrow midlateral black stripe or row of small black spots; males with a large orange, black, and white blotch anteriorly on side of body; body very elongate. Attains about 20 inches (51 cm). Indo-Pacific; a shallow-water species more often found on weedy bottoms with heavy growths of algae than on coral reefs.

Male ⇑   ⇓ Female

FLAME WRASSE   *Cirrhilabrus jordani*   Snyder, 1904
Males bright red dorsally on body, dorsal fin, and caudal fin, shading through yellow to white on chest and lower head; upper part of head with yellow and red bands; females red, the median fins mainly pale yellowish. Largest, 4 inches (10 cm). Hawaiian Islands, generally at depths greater than 60 feet (18 m). Feeds on zooplankton; males maintain large harems.

Lined Coris (Male). See the description on the next page.

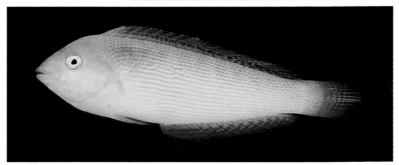

⇑ Female

LINED CORIS malamalama

Coris ballieui Vaillant & Sauvage, 1875

Body of males yellowish to pale pink with narrow blue stripes or rows of blue spots, the head with irregular blue bands; a blackish bar anteriorly on upper side; females white with pink lines; juveniles with an orange-yellow stripe which may persist as one or more anterior blotches on females. To 12 inches (30 cm). Hawaiian Islands, below 60 feet (18 m), on mixed sand and rock bottom.

⇑ Juvenile

Yellowstriped Coris (Male). See description on the next page.

Yellowstriped Coris (Female). See description on the next page.

YELLOWSTRIPED CORIS   hilu

Coris flavovittata (Bennett, 1829)

Body of males light blue-green, strongly mottled
with yellowish brown; head pale blue with numerous irregular reddish spots and a blue and
black spot on opercular flap; females whitish, the
upper third black with 2 narrow yellow stripes;
juveniles black with narrow yellow stripes.
Reaches 20 inches (18 cm); Hawaiian Islands; not
common in the main islands. *Coris lepomis*
Jenkins and *Julis eydouxii* Valenciennes are synonyms based on the male and female forms, respectively. This species was originally described
from a juvenile 3.5 inches in total length.

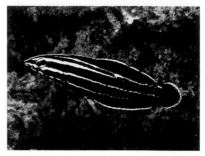

⇑ Juvenile

Yellowtail Coris (Male). See description on the next page.

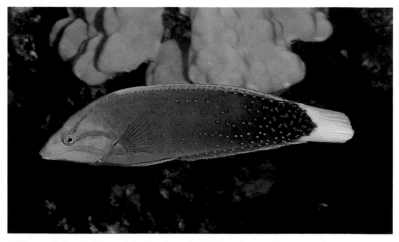

Yellowtail Coris (Female). See description on the next page.

YELLOWTAIL CORIS   hinālea 'akilolo

Coris gaimard (Quoy & Gaimard, 1824)

Body reddish to greenish brown with small bright blue spots (more numerous posteriorly); head with irregular green bands; caudal fin yellow; males with a green to yellowish bar anteriorly on body; juveniles red with 3 large black-edged white spots dorsally on body and 2 smaller ones on head. Reaches 15 inches (38 cm). Central and western Pacific to Christmas Island, eastern Indian Ocean.

⇑ Juvenile

Male ⇑   ⇓ Female

ELEGANT CORIS

Coris venusta Vaillant & Sauvage, 1875

Females yellowish with rose red stripes anteriorly and irregular blue-green bars and spots posteriorly; opercular flap with a red, yellow, and black spot; males similar but more green, the head red with green bands; juveniles with a dark brown stripe on head and anterior body. Largest, 7.6 inches (19.4 cm). Hawaiian Islands; a common inshore reef species.

⇑ Juvenile

Male ⇧　　　　　　　　　　　　　　　　　　　　　　⇩ **Female**

HAWAIIAN KNIFEFISH　*Cymolutes lecluse* (Quoy & Gaimard, 1824)
Males pale greenish, shading to white ventrally, with a very small blue-edged black spot on side above pectoral-fin tip; females with a small blue-edged black spot at upper base of caudal fin; body compressed, more slender than the species of razorfishes; head profile convex. Attains about 8 inches (20 cm). Hawaiian Islands; lives on open sand bottoms; able to dive into sand with the approach of danger.

Bird Wrasse (Male). See description on the next page.

Female ⇧

BIRD WRASSE hinālea 'i'iwi

Gomphosus varius Lacepède, 1801

Males deep blue-green with a vertical reddish line on each scale and a greenish yellow bar above pectoral-fin base; females white anteriorly with a black spot on each scale, gradually becoming dark gray posteriorly, the scales rimmed with black; upper part of snout orange; snout of adults very long and slender. Largest, 12.5 inches (32 cm). Central and western Pacific. Feeds mainly on small benthic crustaceans.

⇧ Juvenile

ORNATE WRASSE 'ōhua *Halichoeres ornatissimus* (Garrett, 1863)
Rose red with a green spot on each scale, the head with green bands and a black and green spot behind eye; small juveniles with 2 green-edged black spots in soft portion of dorsal fin; with growth the more posterior spot disappears first. Attains 6 inches (15 cm). Central and western Pacific; a common inshore species in Hawai'i. Feeds primarily on small mollusks and crustaceans.

HAWAIIAN CLEANER WRASSE *Labroides phthirophagus* Randall, 1958
Yellow anteriorly with a median dorsal black stripe on head and a lateral black stripe that gradually widens posteriorly; upper and lower edges of caudal peduncle and fin magenta; dorsal and anal fins mainly blue; juveniles black with a broad purple to blue stripe on back. Largest, 4 inches (10 cm). Hawaiian Islands. Establishes cleaning stations to which fishes come to have their ectoparasites removed.

SHORTNOSE WRASSE *Macropharyngodon geoffroy* (Quoy & Gaimard, 1824)
Orange-yellow with a dark-edged blue spot on each scale, and blue spots on median fins; males with narrow irregular blue lines on head instead of spots, red above 2 black spots anteriorly in dorsal fin, and a black bar at pectoral-fin base. Largest, 6.2 inches (16 cm). Hawaiian Islands. Feeds primarily on mollusks, which it crushes with its strong pharyngeal teeth, and Foraminifera. *Macropharngodon aquilolo* Jenkins in a synonym. The generic name is in reference to the large pharyngeal molars.

ROCKMOVER WRASSE

Novaculichthys taeniourus (Lacepède, 1801)

Body dark brown with a vertically elongate whitish spot on each scale, the abdomen red with whitish scale edges; head light gray with narrow dark bands radiating from eye; a broad white bar near base of caudal fin; juveniles green, reddish, or brown with dark-edged white blotches and narrow dark bars, the first 2 dorsal spines elongate. To 12 inches (30 cm). Indo-Pacific and tropical eastern Pacific. The young mimic drifting algae.

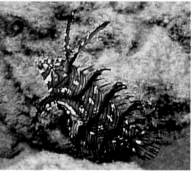

⇑ **Juvenile**

WOOD'S WRASSE *Novaculichthys woodi* Jenkins, 1900
Pale greenish gray (more red in deeper water), becoming pink with white lines on abdomen; a black spot on each membrane of spinous part of dorsal fin; iris red; young with an orange stripe on upper side; body compressed; first dorsal spine flexible. Attains about 7 inches (18 cm). Central and western Pacific. Lives over open sand; dives into sand when alarmed. *N. entargyreus* Jenkins and *N. tatoo* Seale are synonyms.

Male ⇑   ⇓ Female

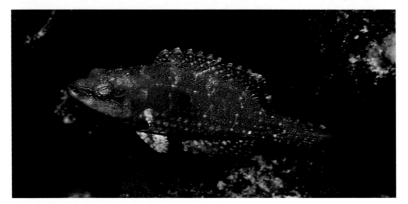

TWOSPOT WRASSE   *Oxycheilinus bimaculatus* (Valenciennes, 1840)
Males light green or greenish brown, the scales edged with orange anteriorly on side of body; a small black spot above pectoral fin; orange lines on head; a deep blue spot on first membrane of dorsal fin with a red and yellow spot above; caudal fin rhomboid with prolonged upper ray; females similar, red with small whitish blotches and flecks. To 6 inches (15 cm). Indo-Pacific; generally on rubble or rubble-sand in over 50 feet (15 m). A common fish but easily overlooked due to small size and secretive habits.

Ringtail Wrasse (Color phase). See description on the next page.

RINGTAIL WRASSE **po'ou** *Oxycheilinus unifasciatus* (Streets, 1877)
Body greenish with an orange to dark reddish bar on each scale except ventrally, a narrow white bar anteriorly on caudal peduncle, and often with a dark lateral stripe; very changeable in color. Largest, 18 inches (46 cm). Central and western Pacific, from 30-584 feet (10-165 m). Feeds on fishes (65% of diet), crabs, brittle stars, and sea urchins. Has caused ciguatera poisoning in Hawai'i.

DISAPPEARING WRASSE *Pseudocheilinus evanidus* Jordan & Evermann, 1903
Red with thin whitish longitudinal lines following scale rows; a bluish white streak on head below eye. Reaches 3.2 inches (8 cm). Indo-Pacific. Occurs in rich coral areas, generally in more than 40 feet (12 m). Very secretive, like others of the genus.

EIGHTSTRIPE WRASSE *Pseudocheilinus octotaenia* Jenkins, 1901
Orange-yellow to pink with 8 narrow dark brown to black stripes on body; median fins and lower part of head with small yellow spots. Largest, 5.3 inches (13.5 cm). Indo-Pacific; some variation in color over its range. Feeds mainly on small benthic crustaceans, sometimes on small mollusks and sea urchins.

FOURSTRIPE WRASSE   *Pseudocheilinus tetrataenia* Schultz, 1960
Orangish dorsally, greenish below, with 4 black-edged blue lines on upper half of body which continue onto postorbital head; a narrow pale blue band from below eye to front of abdomen. Largest, 2.7 inches (7 cm). Central and western Pacific. Never far from shelter, generally in branching coral; remains only fleetingly in the open; hence difficult to photograph underwater.

Male ⇑   ⇓ **Female**

SMALLTAIL WRASSE   *Pseudojuloides cerasinus* (Snyder, 1904)
Males green dorsally on body, light blue ventrally, with a lateral yellow stripe broadly edged above with blue; a large blue-edged dark area in outer part of caudal fin; females red, shading to white on lower head and abdomen and to yellow on snout; body elongate; caudal fin short; teeth on side of jaws nearly incisiform. Largest, 4.8 inches (12 cm). Indo-Pacific and tropical eastern Pacific; usually over coral rubble in more than 60 feet (18 m); closely oriented to the substratum.

Terminal Phase Male ⇑   ⇓ Initial Phase

BELTED WRASSE **'ōmaka** *Stethojulis balteata* (Quoy & Gaimard, 1824)
Terminal males green with a broad blue-edged orange stripe on lower side and blue lines on head, one continuing along back, and orange dorsal fin; initial phase gray-brown, finely dotted dorsally with pale green, with 2 small pale-edged black spots on side of caudal peduncle and a yellow spot above pectoral-fin base. Reaches 6 inches (15 cm). Hawaiian Islands; a common, very active, inshore species.

Blacktail Wrasse (Terminal phase male). See description on the next page.

Initial Phase ⇑

BLACKTAIL WRASSE   hinālea lauhine

Thalassoma ballieui (Vaillant & Sauvage, 1875).

Body of terminal males yellowish with a vertical red line on each scale, the head and chest gray; posterior caudal peduncle and caudal fin blackish; initial phase brownish gray with a maroon line on each scale; juveniles yellowish green with red lines on scales. Largest, 15.5 inches (39.5 cm). Hawaiian Islands. Feeds mainly on sea urchins, crabs, and small fishes. More common in Northwestern Hawaiian Islands than the main islands.

⇑ Juvenile

Saddle Wrasse (Terminal phase male). See description on the next page.

SADDLE WRASSE **hinālea lauwili**

Thalassoma duperrey (Quoy & Gaimard, 1824)

Body green with numerous vertical magenta lines and a broad orange bar anteriorly; head dark purplish gray, shading to green ventrally; terminal males with a whitish bar behind orange bar; juveniles with a black stripe separated by a white band from a lower orange-yellow stripe. Attains 10 inches (25.5 cm). Hawaiian Islands; the most common reef fish in the islands. Feeds principally on crustaceans, mollusks, pelecypods and other worms, brittle stars, sea urchins, and heart urchins.

⇑ Juvenile

Terminal phase male ⇑　　　⇓ Initial phase

SUNSET WRASSE *Thalassoma lutescens* (Lay & Bennett, 1839)
Body of terminal males blue or blue-green anteriorly, shading through green to greenish yellow, with magenta to purple vertical lines; head rose red with narrow green bands; initial phase yellow with vertical orange-red lines on body. Largest, 9.7 inches (24.7 cm). Indo-Pacific; rare in Hawai'i but common at Johnston Island. Hybridizes with the Saddle Wrasse , *T. duperrey* (see figure on p. 122).

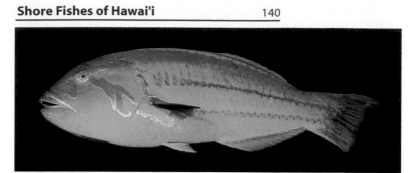

Terminal phase male ⇑   ⇓ Initial phase

SURGE WRASSE   hou   *Thalassoma purpureum* (Forsskål, 1775)
Terminal males blue-green with 3 bright pink stripes on body linked by narrow pink bars; head with broad irregular pink bands; initial phase green with numerous small dark reddish brown spots on head and upper body and 2 dark reddish stripes, the upper with numerous dark reddish brown lines extending above and below. To 17 inches (43 cm). Indo-Pacific; occurs on exposed rocky coasts, generally in less than about 7 feet (2 m). The initial phase was described as *Julis umbrostygma* by Rüppell (1835).

FIVESTRIPE WRASSE   *Thalassoma quinquevittatum* (Lay & Bennett, 1839)
Initial phase green with two magenta stripes on upper side of body linked by magenta lines; head magenta with narrow green bands; terminal males with the same basic pattern but more violet, and the green of the body partly replaced by yellow. Attains 6.7 inches (17 cm). Indo-Pacific; rare in Hawai'i. Like the Sunset Wrasse, this species sometimes interbreeds with the Saddle Wrasse *(T. duperrey)*.

Terminal phase male ⇑   ⇓ Initial phase

CHRISTMAS WRASSE '**āwela** *Thalassoma trilobatum* (Lacepède, 1801)
Initial phase almost identical to that of *T. purpureum*; side of snout before eye with a C to oval-shaped pink to maroon mark (in *purpureum,* a vertical line or Y-shaped mark); body of terminal male rose with 2 rows of close-set rectangular green spots on side; head brownish orange. Largest, 12 inches (30 cm). Indo-Pacific; also an inshore species of rocky coast exposed to wave action.

WHITEBANDED SHARPNOSE WRASSE *Wetmorella albofasciata* Schultz and Marshall, 1954. Reddish brown with 3 narrow white bands on body and 3 white lines radiating from eye; a large black spot between pelvic fins and one on soft portion of dorsal, anal, and pelvic fins; snout pointed. Largest, 2.2 inches (5.5 cm). Indo-Pacific. Usually hides in the deeper recesses of caves, hence rarely seen.

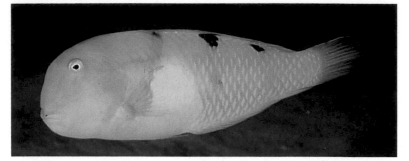

WHITEPATCH RAZORFISH   **laenihi**   *Xyrichtys aneitensis* (Günther, 1862)
Light gray with a large white patch on side of body centered on pectoral-fin tip; a dusky area in front of patch in female, yellow in male; 3 faint dusky bars on body (darker in juveniles), each ending dorsally in a blackish spot; first 2 dorsal spines flexible, nearly separated from rest of fin, and not elevated. Reaches 8 inches (20 cm). Central and western Pacific, over open sand bottom; like others of the genus, may dive into sand when alarmed. Males maintain a harem of females.

BALDWIN'S RAZORFISH   **laenihi**   *Xyrichtys baldwini* (Jordan & Evermann, 1903)
Light gray with a bluish white patch (about 3 scales in height) centered on pectoral tip and preceded by yellow; a large black spot above white patch (mixed with red in males); males with a black spot posteriorly in anal fin; dorsal fin as in *X. aneitensis.* Largest, 9.5 inches (24 cm). Hawaiian Islands, Japan and Taiwan. Lives over open sand; difficult to approach. *X. evides* Jordan & Richardson is a synonym.

Peacock Razorfish. See description on the next page.

PEACOCK RAZORFISH   laenihi

Xyrichtys pavo Valenciennes, 1840

Gray with 2 large yellowish white areas on lower side and one on caudal peduncle; a small black spot, edged anteriorly in pale blue, above eighth lateral-line scale; one color phase nearly black; first 2 dorsal spines completely separate from rest of fin and elongate (more so in juveniles). To at least 12 inches (30 cm). Indo-Pacific. The juvenile stage mimics drifting leaves; its long first two dorsal spines are held forward like the stem.

⇑ Juvenile

BLACKSIDE RAZORFISH   laenihi   *Xyrichtys umbrilatus* (Jenkins, 1900)
Light gray with a large black blotch (largest in males) on side of body below and above end of pectoral fin, the scales around lower part of blotch bluish with white edges; juveniles with black bars; forehead very steep, like others of the genus; first 2 dorsal spines flexible and nearly separate from rest of fin, but not elongate in adults. Reaches 9 inches (23 cm). Known only from the Hawaiian Islands.

PARROTFISHES (SCARIDAE)

The common name parrotfishes for this family is well chosen because of the bright colors of most species and the beak-like dentition formed by the fusion of teeth. Also unique is the pharyngeal dentition which consists of series of molariform teeth on upper and lower bony plates at the back of the throat, the upper convex, the lower concave. Parrotfishes lack a true stomach and have a very long intestine. All have a single unnotched dorsal fin of IX, 10 rays, and an anal fin of III, 9 rays. Like the wrasses from which parrotfishes are believed to have evolved, the juveniles are often very different in color from the adults, and there are usually two strikingly different color patterns associated with sex. Most species undergo sex reversal from female to male as they change color from a drab phase (generally gray or reddish brown, termed the initial phase) to a more gaudy color phase (usually dominated by green or blue-green, called the terminal male). Some species are both female and male in the initial phase; spawning in this phase occurs in aggregations dominated by males. Others are only female in the initial phase. Terminal males tend to establish sexual territories in which they maintain a harem of females; they court and spawn with individual females. Parrotfishes feed by grazing on algae from rock surfaces; when the surface is dead coral, they scrape into the limestone. Some species take algae growing on the surface of sand, ingesting sand at the same time. A few of the larger species feed in part on live coral (leaving a characteristic mark showing the median suture of the dental plates). The algae, along with

Subadults of Palenose Parrotfish

the bits of rock, coral, and sand, is triturated in the pharyngeal mill, making it more digestible. In the process, limestone rock fragments are ground into sand, and sand into finer sand. Parrotfishes, therefore, are a major producer of sand in coral-reef areas.

Stareye Parrotfish (Terminal phase male). See description on the next page.

Initial phase ⇑

STAREYE PARROTFISH   pōnuhunuhu   *Calotomus carolinus* (Valenciennes, 1840)
Males dull blue-green with a vertical dark pink line on each scale and pink bands radiating from eye; females mottled orangish brown, shading to orange-pink ventrally; teeth not fully fused, still visible on outer surface of dental plates; pectoral rays 13. Attains 20 inches (50 cm). Indo-Pacific and tropical eastern Pacific. *Calotomus sandwicensis* (Valenciennes) is a synonym.

Male ⇑   ⇓ Female

YELLOWBAR PARROTFISH   *Calotomus zonarchus* (Jenkins, 1903)
Males gray with a broad yellow bar (containing a few white scales) in middle of body and irregular deep pink bars on head below level of mouth; females light gray to light reddish brown with a few whitish to pale pink scales on body; head finely dotted with whitish; dentition like *C. carolinus;* pectoral rays 13. Reaches 12 inches (30 cm). Hawaiian Islands; rare except in Northwestern Hawaiian Islands.

Terminal phase male ⇑   ⇓ Initial phase

SPECTACLED PARROTFISH   uhu uliuli, uhu 'ahu'ula   *Chlorurus perspicillatus* (Steindachner, 1879) Terminal males (**uhu uliuli**) blue-green with orange-pink dots anteriorly and orange-pink edges on scales posteriorly; head in front of eye lavender with a blue-edged bar across forehead; initial phase (**uhu 'ahu'ula**) dark reddish brown with red fins and a broad white bar at base of caudal fin. Attains 24 inches (61 cm). Hawaiian Islands. Formerly classified in *Scarus. Callyodon ahula* Jenkins is a synonym. Initial phase sometimes seen in aggregations.

Bullethead Parrotfish (Terminal phase male). See description on the next page.

Initial phase ⇑

BULLETHEAD PARROTFISH   uhu

Chlorurus sordidus (Forsskål, 1775)

Terminal males mainly green, with a vertical pink line on scales, usually with a suffusion of yellow over most of side of body; dental plates blue-green; initial phase dark brown, becoming red at front of head; able to turn on a double row of whitish spots or a broad pale bar at base of caudal fin containing a large dark spot; dental plates white; caudal fin truncate. To 16 inches (40 cm). Indo-Pacific.

⇑ Juvenile

Regal Parrotfish (Terminal phase male). See description on the next page.

Initial phase ⇑

REGAL PARROTFISH **lauia** *Scarus dubius* Bennett, 1828
Terminal males orange-pink with a vertically elongate blue-green spot on scales and narrow blue-green bands on head; initial phase brownish red, becoming red on lower part of head, with 2 or 3 narrow pale stripes on abdomen; pectoral rays usually 14 (15 in the above species of *Chlorurus*). To 14 inches (35.5 cm). Hawaiian Islands. More common in the Northwestern Hawaiian Islands than in the main islands.

Palenose Parrotfish (Terminal phase male). See description on the next page.

Palenose Parrotfish (Initial phase). See description on the next page.

PALENOSE PARROTFISH uhu

Scarus psittacus Forsskål, 1775.

Terminal males green with an orange-pink bar at edge of scales; dorsal part of snout lavender; a yellow area often on side of caudal peduncle; initial phase reddish to grayish brown; front of snout paler than rest of head; a small black spot at upper base of pectoral fins, and a dark spot on first membrane of dorsal fin; pectoral rays 14. To 12 inches (30 cm). Indo-Pacific; common in the Hawaiian Islands. Initial phase often seen in small schools. First described from the Red Sea.

⇑ Juvenile

Terminal phase male. ⇑   ⇓ Initial phase

REDLIP PARROTFISH   pālukaluka   *Scarus rubroviolaceus* Bleeker, 1849
Terminal male green, the scale edges salmon pink; dental plates blue-green; initial phase gray to reddish brown with small black spots and irregular lines on scales; head red, brightest on lips; fins red; head and anterior body often abruptly darker than posterior body; dental plates white; dorsal profile of snout initially nearly vertical; caudal fin of adults lunate; pectoral rays 15. Largest examined, 28 inches (71 cm). Indo-Pacific and tropical eastern Pacific. *Scarus jordani* (Jenkins) is one of nine synonyms.

SANDLANCES (AMMODYTIDAE)

The fishes of this family live in schools over sand and readily dive into the sand when approached, hence the common name sandlance. They are small and slender-bodied; the pointed lower jaw projects beyond the upper. There are no teeth in jaws and no swimbladder. The caudal fin is forked. The dorsal fin is very long, with 40-69 soft rays. Three species are known from Hawai'i, but two occur at depths not reached by SCUBA divers.

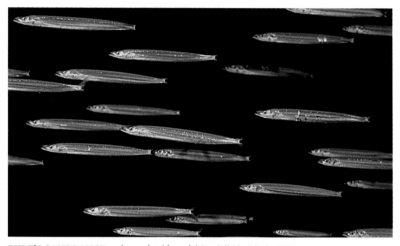

PYLE'S SANDLANCE   *Ammodytoides pylei* Randall, Ida & Earle, 1994
Lavender-brown dorsally, soon shading to silvery white; a series of small blackish spots at outer edge of dorsal fin; dorsal rays 48-52; scales small, in straight diagonal rows. Largest, 6.6 inches (16.7 cm). Hawaiian Islands; over sand from 7-120 m. Occurs in loose aggregations while feeding on zooplankton; forms swift-swimming schools when approached. Spawning was observed shortly before sunset.

DRAGONETS (CALLIONYMIDAE)

This is a large family of small bottom-dwelling fishes that have a strong spine on the corner of the preopercle which usually bears barb-like spinules. The head is broad and depressed; the body is moderately elongate and somewhat depressed; there are no scales; the mouth is small, and the upper jaw is very protrusible; the gill opening is small and dorsal in position. There are 2 dorsal fins (except species of *Draculo* which have only a soft dorsal), the first of IV spines and the second of 6-10 soft rays. The innermost pelvic ray is joined by membrane to the pectoral fins. Males often have a higher first dorsal fin than females and are usually more colorful. Pair spawning has been observed; the eggs are pelagic. Most species live on sand or mud bottoms; some can bury quickly in the sediment. Eight species are known from Hawai'i.

Male ⇑   ⇓ Female

LONGTAIL DRAGONET   *Callionymus decoratus* (Gilbert, 1905)
Light brown with numerous dark circles and some small dark brown blotches; first dorsal fin of male
with a large and a small black spot (female with one); first spine of dorsal fin of male filamentous; caudal
fin of male longer than body, of female about half body length; upper margin of preopercular spine
serrate. To 11 inches (28 cm). Hawaiian Islands; on sand from the shallows to 360 feet (110 m).

Male ⇑   ⇑ Female

EXCLAMATION POINT DRAGONET   *Synchiropus corallinus* Gilbert, 1905
Males with blue dots on head; first dorsal fin of males twice height of second (slightly higher than second in female), with 3-6 narrow vertical black bars and black spots at the base (hence appearing like a
series of exclamation points); outer half of anal fin black; females finely mottled, often red on first
dorsal fin and a broad area beneath; preopercular spine with 6 upper spinules including tip, and a lower
antrorse spine at base. Attains 1.5 inches (3.8 cm). Hawai'i and Japan in 39-400 feet (12-122 m).

SANDPERCHES (PINGUIPEDIDAE)

This small family of four genera is represented in the warm-water Indo-Pacific region only by the genus *Parapercis*. The species of this genus are moderately elongate and little compressed, with eyes that are oriented as much upward as to the side; there are 2 dorsal fins, the first of IV or V spines and the second of 20-24 soft rays. These fishes are usually found on rubble or sand bottoms in the vicinity of reefs; they rest upon the bottom, propping themselves with their well-separated pelvic fins. All are carnivorous, feeding mainly on benthic crustaceans, occasionally on small fishes. Many show sexual color differences; sex reversal from female to male has been demonstrated for some species. It is expected that all will prove to be hermaphroditic. The family was known as Parapercidae or Mugiloididae in the older literature. Two species occur in Hawai'i, one of which is known only from deep water.

REDSPOTTED SANDPERCH *Parapercis schauinslandii* (Steindachner, 1900)
White with 2 longitudinal rows of squarish red spots on body; first dorsal fin red with a large black spot basally in center of fin; dorsal rays V,21; 6 canine teeth at front of lower jaw; caudal fin emarginate. Reaches 5 inches (13 cm). Indo-Pacific; occurs on rubble-sand substrata, usually at depths greater than 50 feet (15 m). Easily approached underwater.

TRIPLEFINS (TRIPTERYGIIDAE)

This is a large family of small fishes (usually 1-2 inches; 2.5-5 cm) that have 3 separate dorsal fins, the first usually of III or IV spines, the second of VIII to XVI spines, and the third of 7 to 17 soft rays. They live on coral reefs or rocky bottom, often with a heavy growth of algae. Because of their mottled color pattern, small size, and cryptic habits, they are often overlooked. They feed on small invertebrates and algae. Species of triplefins occur from cold temperate to tropic seas. Only one species is known from Hawaiian waters.

Male ⇑   ⇑ Female

HAWAIIAN TRIPLEFIN   *Enneapterygius atriceps* (Jenkins, 1903)
Males gray, the scale edges red, with irregular dark brown and white bars; lower two-thirds of head black; females lack red edges on scales and black on head; dorsal rays III + XIII-XIV + 8-10. Rarely exceeds 1.2 inches (3 cm). Hawaiian Islands; common but not often seen because of its small size and secretive habits. Sometimes classified in *Tripterygion*.

BLENNIES (BLENNIIDAE)

The blennies are a large family (over 300 species) of small, agile, bottom-dwelling fishes. All lack scales, and all have their pelvic fins clearly anterior to the pectorals, with an indistinct spine and 2-4 soft rays. Most are blunt-headed, and many have small tentacles or cirri on the head; some have a median fleshy crest dorsally on the head. There is a continuous dorsal fin with III-XVII flexible spines; there may be a notch between the spinous and soft portions. All have II spines in the anal fin; these are capped with fleshy knobs in males, and the first is hidden by tissue in fe-

Bullethead Rockskipper

males. The species of the genera *Omobranchus* and *Plagiotremus* have a pair of enormous curved canine teeth at the front of the lower jaw.

Some blennies, such as those of the genera *Istiblennius* and *Entomacrodus*, live inshore on rocky bottom exposed to surge; they are able to leap from pool to pool, hence are often called rockskippers. Blennies tend to take refuge in small holes in the reef into which they back tail-first. Most tropical species graze on benthic algae; the Shortbodied Blenny (*Exallias brevis*) is unusual in feeding on coral polyps. The fangblennies of the genus *Plagiotremus* make rapid attacks on other fishes to remove mucus and skin tissue (sometimes with small scales); they do this with their small anterior incisiform teeth, not the large canines (which are used in defense). Fangblennies often direct their attacks to divers, but one feels only a light touch when they make contact.

The blennies for which the reproductive habits are known lay demersal eggs that are guarded by the male parent. Fourteen species are recorded from the Hawaiian Islands. One of these, the wide-ranging *Ecsenius bicolor*, was found in Pearl Harbor in 1950 on a drydock towed from Guam; it has not been seen in Hawai'i since. The general Hawaiian name for blennies is **pāo'o**.

BULLETHEAD ROCKSKIPPER   *Blenniella gibbifrons* (Quoy & Gaimard, 1824)
Body of males with 7 double, interconnected, dark gray-brown bars and numerous small light blue-green spots, those on head small; females pale greenish with 2 dark stripes which may break up into double spots; red dots on head; a black spot on first membrane of dorsal fin of both sexes. Largest, 5 inches (12.5 cm). Islands of the Pacific Plate and western Indian Ocean, usually in less than 6 feet (1.8 m).

GARGANTUAN BLENNY   *Cirripectes obscurus* (Borodin, 1927)
Dark brown with white dots on head and anterior body; a small black spot often behind eye; fringe of cirri on nape black; males develop a red head during spawning time; dorsal soft rays 15-17 (usually 16); cirri on nape 36-47. Largest, 7.6 inches (19.3 cm), from Midway. Hawaiian Islands; occurs along rocky shores exposed to wave action. Like others of the genus, quickly hides in holes when approached.

DOTTED-LINE BLENNY *Cirripectes quagga* (Fowler & Ball, 1924)
Color variable; in Hawai'i usually dark brown with vertical rows of very small white spots on body (4 or 5 spots per row); dorsal soft rays 14-16 (usually 15); cirri on nape 23-36 (usually 26-32). Largest, 3.5 inches (8.9 cm). Indo-Pacific, generally in less than 30 feet (9.2 m). Away from Hawai'i, usually with dark bars on body, sometimes with a broad red or yellow area posteriorly.

SCARFACE BLENNY *Cirripectes vanderbilti* (Fowler, 1938)
Dark brown, often with small bright red spots and short irregular lines on head; a bright red ring in outer part of iris; fringe of cirri on nape black; dorsal soft rays 13-15 (usually 14); cirri on nape 31-42; lower lip smooth. Largest, 4.4 inches (11.3 cm). Hawaiian Islands; known from the depth range of 3-36 feet (1-11 m); the most frequently seen species of the genus in Hawai'i. Closely related to *C. variolosus* (Valenciennes) from elsewhere in the Indo-Pacific (both occur at Johnston Island).

MARBLED BLENNY **pāo'o** *Entomacrodus marmoratus* (Bennett, 1828)
Pale greenish, spotted and barred with dark brownish gray, the darkest spot on shoulder; dorsal soft rays usually 15 or 16; a long tentacle over eye with fine side branches; 2 small cirri on each side of nape (medial one branched). Attains nearly 6 inches (15 cm). Hawaiian Islands; occurs along rocky shores exposed to surf, often in the intertidal zone.

STRASBURG'S BLENNY   *Entomacrodus strasburgi* Springer, 1967
Greenish with 6 double dark gray-brown bars on body, 3 rows of whitish spots (most horizontally elongate), and dull orange markings on head; dorsal soft rays 13-15; tentacle over eye with 1-4 long branches (usually 3 in adults); one cirrus on each side of nape. Largest, 1.9 inches (4.8 cm). Hawaiian Islands; occurs along wave-swept rocky shores in less than 3 feet (0.9 m).

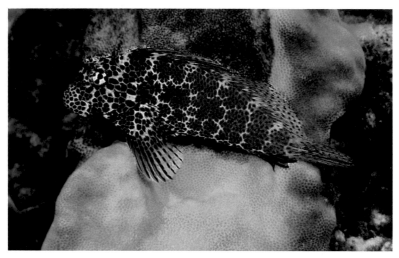

Shortbodied Blenny (Male, over yellow ova). See description on the next page.

Shortbodied Blenny (Female). See description on the next page.

SHORTBODIED BLENNY   pāo'o kauila   *Exallias brevis* (Kner, 1868)
Males whitish with numerous close-set dark brown spots on head and anterior body, the spots becoming red and clumping to form still larger spots posteriorly on body; dorsal and caudal fins red with small dark spots; females without red coloration; body deep for a blenny; a fringe of cirri on nape. To 6 inches (15 cm). Indo-Pacific; feeds on coral polyps. Eggs bright yellow, rarely eaten by other fishes.

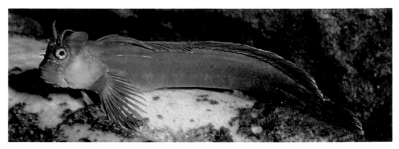

ZEBRA ROCKSKIPPER   pāo'o   *Istiblennius zebra*   (Vaillant & Sauvage, 1875)
Color varying from nearly black to gray or tan, usually with dark double bars on side of body; a median fleshy crest on head (larger in males); a long unbranched tentacle over eye; no cirri on nape. Largest, 7.6 inches (19.3 cm), from Laysan. Hawaiian Islands. Occurs on exposed rocky shores from the highest tidepools to the surf zone. Remarkable for its ability to leap from pool to pool.

ROUNDHEAD BLENNY   *Omobranchus rotundiceps* (Macleay, 1881)
Gray to tan with oblique dark brown bands or rows of spots anteriorly on body and chevron-like bands posteriorly, with narrow white bands between; a large black spot behind eye; no crest on head; dorsal rays usually XII,18-20. Largest, 2.8 inches (7.1 cm). One subspecies from Hawai'i and Samoa to Nicobar Islands, a second from Australia. Marine to brackish, inshore on rocky substrata in protected localities.

Tasseled Blenny. See description on the next page.

TASSELED BLENNY   *Parablennius thysanius* (Jordan & Seale, 1907)
Brown with 7 sets of 4 blackish spots along back; often with a midlateral row of blackish dots; head and chest with orangish brown dots; tentacle over eye palmate with 4-6 cirri in females, as many as 22 in males; dorsal rays XII,14-15. Reaches 2 inches (5 cm). Philippines to Persian Gulf; probably unintentionally introduced to Hawai'i (most likely in ship's ballast water). The illustrated specimen was collected from a mooring line in Kāne'ohe Bay, O'ahu.

EWA FANGBLENNY   *Plagiotremus ewaensis* (Brock, 1948).
Color varies from orange with 2 dark-edged bright blue stripes to dark brown with 2 blue stripes; body very slender; snout overhanging ventral mouth; 2 huge curved canine teeth in lower jaw; dorsal rays X-XII,34-36. Attains 4 inches (10 cm). Hawaiian Islands; perhaps only subspecifically different from the Indo-Pacific *P. rhinorhynchos* (Bleeker). Feeds on mucus and skin tissue of other fishes.

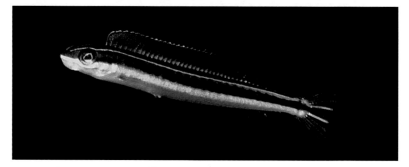

GOSLINE'S FANGBLENNY   *Plagiotremus goslinei* (Strasburg, 1959)
A gray to reddish brown stripe on side, bordered narrowly above and broadly below by pale blue or yellow, and containing a series of close-set black bars; body slender; snout overhanging ventral mouth; 2 huge curved canines in lower jaw; dorsal rays VII-VIII,34-37. To 2.4 inches (6 cm). Hawaiian Islands; very closely related to the Indo-Pacific *P. tapeinosoma*. Feeds on mucus and skin tissue of other fishes.

GOBIES (GOBIIDAE)

The Gobiidae is the largest family of marine fishes in the world, and there are many species that live in freshwater environments. About 1,875 species are known; still more remain to be described. Although the third largest family of fishes in Hawai'i, with 28 marine species, it is poorly represented compared to other areas of the Indo-Pacific. This is probably due to the relatively short larval life of most species. The majority of gobies are small, most less than 10 cm in length [and a few as small as 0.4 inches (1 cm) as adults—the smallest fishes in the world]. The pelvic fins of gobies are close together and usually fused to form a sucking disk. Nearly all the species have 2 dorsal fins, the first often with VI spines; most have a rounded caudal fin. Scales are present on the body of most species, but a few lack scales; there is no lateral line. The opercle is without a spine.

Gobies are primarily shallow-water species; all are carnivorous and bottom-dwelling. Some occur only in tidepools or on very shallow sand or mud flats, hence they are not often seen by snorkelers or divers; examples are the frill gobies of the genus *Bathygobius* of which three occur in Hawai'i (only one common species of the genus discussed below). Most gobies rest directly on the substratum, but some hover a short distance above. Gobies are associated with a variety of habitats such as coral reef, sand, mud, rubble, or seagrass. Many live in close association with other animals such as sponges, gorgonians, and snapping shrimps. Nearly all gobies for which the reproductive habits are known lay demersal eggs which are guarded by the male parent. A few have been shown to be protogynous hermaphrodites (begin mature life as females and change sex later to males). The general Hawaiian name for gobies is **'o'opu**.

A pair of Hawaiian Shrimp Gobies with symbiotic snapping shrimp.

The Hawaiian marine gobies not treated below include three above-mentioned species of *Bathygobius*, *Bryaninops tigris*, *Cabillus* sp. (undescribed), *Discordipinna griessingeri*, two new species of *Eviota*, *Kelloggella oligolepis*, *Mugilogobius cavifrons* (accidentally introduced), *Oxyurichthys lonchotus*, *Oxyurichthys* sp. (new from deep water), *Priolepis farcimen*, and *Trimma unisquamis*. None of these species are apt to be seen by divers or snorkelers.

HALFSPOTTED GOBY

Asterropteryx semipunctatus Rüppell, 1830

Dark to light gray, often with a broad blackish stripe from eye to caudal-fin base; numerous bright blue dots on head and body, mostly on ventral half; dorsal rays VI - I, 9-11; head scaled except snout and interorbital space; 3-9 spines on edge of preopercle above corner. Reaches 2.5 inches (6.5 cm). Indo-Pacific; usually found in protected waters on silty dead reefs; takes refuge in a hole or burrow. Abundant in Kāne'ohe Bay.

COCOS FRILL GOBY   'o'opu ōhune   *Bathygobius cocosensis* (Bleeker, 1854)
Light gray-brown with broad dark bars on the back and elliptical black spots alternating with smaller spots in a row on lower side of body; dorsal rays usually VI - I,9; pectoral rays 18-20, the upper 3 or 4 free of membrane; predorsal scales to above preopercular margin. To 3.2 inches (8.2 cm). Indo-Pacific; common in tidepools and shallow silty sand flats.

GORGONIAN GOBY

Bryaninops amplus Larson, 1985

Transparent dorsally with 7 faint narrow orange-red bars; ventral half of body red to orangish yellow; an internal silvery white line above vertebral column; dorsal rays usually VI - I,8; pectoral rays 15-17, branched except lower 2; scales about 53. Reaches 2.2 inches (5.6 cm, large for the genus). Indo-Pacific; usually found on gorgonian seawhips, sometimes on mooring lines.

WHIP-CORAL GOBY

Bryaninops yongei (Davis & Cohen, 1968)

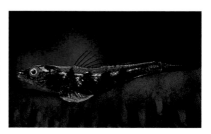

Transparent dorsally with 7 narrow yellowish brown bars that link to ventral dusky yellowish brown half of body; an internal pale yellowish to whitish line above vertebral column; dorsal rays usually VI - I,8-9; pectoral rays usually 15-16, all but lower 3-6 branched; scales about 40. Attains 1.5 inches (3.5 cm). Indo-Pacific; usually found on the antipatharian seawhip *Cirrhipathes anguina*.

HAWAIIAN SAND GOBY

Coryphopterus sp.

Translucent with blackish orange-yellow dots, a black spot smaller than pupil at base of caudal fin, and a vertical blackish line on back extending into first dorsal fin; dorsal and caudal fins with orange-yellow dots; dorsal rays VI - I,9; pectoral rays 18-20. Attains 2.4 inches (6 cm). Hawaiian Islands and Ryukyu Islands; occurs on sand in shallow coral-reef areas. Formerly misidentified as *Fusigobius neophytus* (Günther, 1877).

DIVINE DWARF GOBY

Eviota epiphanes Jenkins, 1903

Translucent with internal dark bars; blackish red bars on head; scales of body rimmed with red; dorsal rays VI - I,8-9 (usually 9); pelvic fins divided, the rays with many lateral branches. Reaches only 0.8 inches (2 cm). Hawaiian Islands, Line Islands, and southern Japan; common on coral reefs but rarely seen due to small size and cryptic habits. Larvae of *Eviota* are more abundant than those of any other shore species in the islands.

EYEBAR GOBY *Gnatholepis anjerensis* (Bleeker, 1850).
Pale gray with dark brown dots dorsally on body, a series of dusky blotches along side with dark dots, a blackish streak extending posterior to eye containing a yellow spot above base of pectoral fin, and a narrow blackish bar below eye; dorsal rays VI - I,11; pectoral rays usually 16; posterior lower lip with a ventral flap. To 3.2 inches (8 cm). Indo-Pacific; common on sand or sand and rubble adjacent to reefs.

CLOUDY GOBY

Hazeus nephodes (E. K. Jordan, 1925)

Light greenish gray with numerous small dark brown spots, scattered irregular whitish blotches, and a midlateral row of double or triple black spots; first spine of both dorsal fins stout and sharp-tipped. Attains 2 inches (5 cm). Known to date only from the Hawaiian Islands and Marshall Islands; occurs on silty sand in protected waters.

MICHEL'S GOBY

Pleurosicya micheli Fourmanoir, 1971

Transparent with an internal red stripe which extends onto lower half of caudal fin; a white or pale pink line along top of vertebral column interrupted by 6 blackish red dashes; body slender; eyes large; dorsolateral in position; dorsal rays usually VI - I,8. Attains 1 inch (2.5 cm). Indo-Pacific; usually found on hard corals; known from depth range of 3-174 feet (1-53 m).

GOLDEN GOBY

Priolepis aureoviridis (Gosline, 1959)

Orange-yellow, the scale edges brown, with narrow gray bars on head and body; fins orange-yellow; dorsal rays VI - I,10-12; scales in longitudinal series on body 29-33; no scales on upper half of operculum; eyes not elevated. Reaches 2.5 inches (6.4 cm). Hawaiian Islands and Caroline Islands. Very secretive in habits; usually in small crevices or holes, often on roof of caves.

NOBLE GOBY

Priolepis eugenius (Jordan & Evermann, 1903)

Dark gray-brown with narrow light gray bars on head and body; median fins dark gray-brown; dorsal rays VI - I,11-12; scales in longitudinal series on body 27-29; upper half of operculum scaled; eyes elevated, the narrow interorbital space deeply concave. Largest, 2.2 inches (5.6 cm). Hawaiian Islands; common in well-developed reefs, but cryptic and rarely seen.

RIMMED-SCALE GOBY

Priolepis limbatosquamis (Gosline, 1959)

Body light gray with faint dusky bars, the edges of the scales narrowly dark orangish brown; head light gray with dark-edged orange bars; dorsal rays VI - I,9-10; scales in longitudinal series 26-27; no scales on operculum; eyes not elevated above dorsal profile. Reaches 1.2 inches (3 cm). Hawaiian Islands, in coral reefs. Very secretive, like others of the genus.

HAWAIIAN SHRIMP GOBY   *Psilogobius mainlandi* Baldwin, 1972
Light gray with numerous small bright blue spots and brownish orange spots; anterior body with vertical pale greenish lines; dorsal rays usually VI - I,10, the first dorsal about twice as high as second. To 2.3 inches (5.8 cm). Hawaiian Islands, on silty sand in shallow protected waters. Lives symbiotically in a burrow with the snapping shrimp *Alpheus rapax;* the shrimp builds and maintains the burrow; the goby is the sentinel; with superior vision and lateralis system, it can detect a predator sooner.

TAYLOR'S GOBY

Trimma taylori Lobel, 1979

Translucent yellow, the scale edges purplish blue; median fins spotted with yellow; paired fins yellow; dorsal rays usually VI - I,10; second dorsal spine long and filamentous in males. Largest, 1 inch (2.5 cm). Hawai'i to western Indian Ocean; first found at O'ahu; occurs in aggregations in small caves at depths of 10 to 165 feet (3-50 m).

DARTFISHES AND WORMFISHES (MICRODESMIDAE)

This family once included just the wormfishes, but the dartfishes (sometimes known as hover gobies) have now been shifted from the Gobiidae to this family. All microdesmids have elongate compressed bodies (those of the wormfishes extremely elongate). The scales are very small and usually nonoverlapping; there is no lateral line. The mouth is oblique with a heavy protruding lower jaw. The pelvic fins are separate, with one spine and 2-4 soft rays. Most of these fishes live over sand,

Juveniles of the Spottail Dartfish

rubble, or mud bottoms and take refuge in burrows. Often a pair of adults or several juveniles will occupy the same burrow. The dartfishes rise well off the bottom to feed on zooplankton. Their common name is derived from how rapidly they dart, head first, into their burrow with the approach of danger.

CURIOUS WORMFISH   *Gunnellichthys curiosus* Dawson, 1968
Light blue (brighter anteriorly) with an orange stripe on body, the stripe becoming dusky orange on head; a black spot on opercle within orange stripe, and a large blue-edged black spot at base of caudal fin; body very elongate; dorsal rays XX-XXI, 40-42. Largest, 4.5 inches (11.5 cm). Indo-Pacific; usually seen over rubble bottoms. Swims in a sinuous manner, usually just above the substratum. Difficult to approach underwater; like dartfishes, it can dive quickly into a burrow when alarmed.

FIRE DARTFISH *Nemateleotris magnifica* Fowler, 1938
Body white anteriorly, shading through red to reddish black on caudal fin; head light yellow anteriorly, grading to white, with a median lavender band; first dorsal fin white, its anterior part extremely elongate; dorsal rays VI - I,28-32. Attains 3.2 inches (8.1 cm). Indo-Pacific; rare in the Hawaiian Islands; often imported from other areas as aquarium fish. Feeds mainly on planktonic crustaceans.

SPOTTAIL DARTFISH *Ptereleotris heteroptera* (Bleeker, 1855)
Light blue to blue-green, shading to whitish on abdomen, with a few iridescent blue-green markings on head; caudal fin whitish to light yellow with a large blackish spot; dorsal rays VI - I,29-33. Largest, 4.7 inches (12 cm). Indo-Pacific; usually seen in pairs over sand or sand-rubble bottoms near reefs; known from depths of 23-150 feet (7-46 m).

MOORISH IDOL FAMILY (ZANCLIDAE)

MOORISH IDOL   kihikihi   *Zanclus cornutus* (Linnaeus, 1758)
The only species of the family; white anteriorly, yellow posteriorly, with 2 broad black bars; a black-edged orange spot dorsally on snout; caudal fin largely black; body very deep and strongly compressed; snout very pointed; dorsal fin very high, the third spine long and filamentous. Reaches 8 inches (20 cm). Indo-Pacific and tropical eastern Pacific. Feeds mainly on sponges, occasionally on algae.

SURGEONFISHES (ACANTHURIDAE)

The Hawaiian fishes of this family are readily identified by having 1 or 2 spines on the side of the caudal peduncle. The species of the genera *Acanthurus*, *Ctenochaetus*, and *Zebrasoma* have a single lancet-like spine which folds into a groove; whereas those of the genus *Naso* have 2 fixed keel-like spines. All surgeonfishes have a deep compressed body with the eye high on the head; the mouth is small with a single row of close-set teeth; the teeth may be spatulate with denticulate edges and fixed in the jaws (as in *Acanthurus*), or numerous, slender with incurved tips, and movable (as in *Ctenochaetus*). There is a single unnotched dorsal fin with IV to IX spines; the anal fin has III spines (except *Naso* with II); the pelvic fins have a spine and 3 or 5 soft rays (3 in *Naso*). Some of the species of *Naso* have a horn-like projection on the forehead, the basis for their common name unicornfishes (others of the genus without the rostral horn are still called unicornfishes).

The species of *Ctenochaetus* and several of *Acanthurus*, such as *A. xanthopterus* and related species, have a thick-walled gizzard-like stomach. All of the surgeonfishes have a very long intestine. Most feed on benthic algae. The species of *Acanthurus* graze principally on filamentous algae; those with gizzard-like stomachs often ingest sand with their algal food to assist in trituration of the algae. Some species of *Acanthurus*, such as *A. triostegus* and *A. leucopareius,* form feeding aggregations to overwhelm territorial herbivorous damselfishes. The algal-feeding species of *Naso*, *N. lituratus* and *N. unicornis,* browse mainly on leafy algae such as *Sargassum*. The species of *Ctenochaetus* feed on detritus and algal fragments which they whisk with their comb-like teeth from the substratum (at the same time employing suction). One Hawaiian species of *Acanthurus* and five of *Naso* feed mainly on zooplankton well above the bottom.

Surgeonfishes are able to slash other fishes (or humans who do not handle them carefully) with their caudal spines by a rapid side-sweep of the tail; some species have bright hues around the caudal spines as warning coloration. Spawning from aggregations has been observed in some species of *Acanthurus*, *Ctenochaetus,* and *Zebrasoma* at dusk (and for some at dawn, hence correlated with low light intensity). The eggs are small and pelagic. The late larval stage is orbicular, transparent with silvery over the abdomen, and small scales in narrow vertical ridges on the body. This stage has venomous second dorsal, second anal, and pelvic spines; these spines remain venomous in the adults of at least some of the species of *Naso*. Twenty-four species of surgeonfishes are recorded from Hawai'i; however, the colorful *Acanthurus lineatus*, is known only from two individuals.

Achilles Tang. See description on the next page.

ACHILLES TANG   pāku'iku'i   *Acanthurus achilles* Shaw, 1803
Black with a large elliptical bright orange spot posteriorly on body enclosing caudal spine (orange spot lacking in juveniles); caudal fin with a broad orange middle zone separated by black from white posterior border; dorsal rays IX,29-33. Largest, 10 inches (25 cm). Islands of Oceania; occurs in moderately turbulent water of exposed reefs. Aggressively territorial.

RINGTAIL SURGEONFISH   pualu   *Acanthurus blochii* Valenciennes, 1835
Dark bluish or greenish gray with small faint yellowish to light gray spots forming irregular longitudinal lines on body; an elongate yellow spot behind eye; a white bar usually across caudal-fin base; dorsal fin dull orange-yellow with 8 or 9 blue bands; dorsal rays IX,25-27. Attains 17 inches (43 cm). Indo-Pacific; feeds more over sandy areas than on reefs.

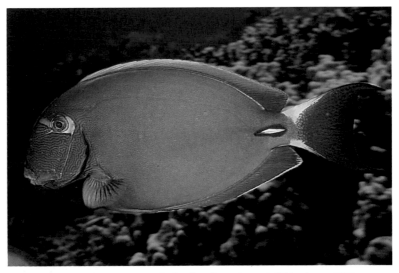

EYESTRIPE SURGEONFISH   palani   *Acanthurus dussumieri* Valenciennes, 1835
Yellowish brown with irregular narrow blue lines on body; head yellowish with blue spots and lines; a broad yellow band across interorbital space, and a yellow spot behind and adjacent to eye; sheath of caudal spine white, the socket edged in black; dorsal and anal fins yellow with a blue band at base; caudal fin blue with small blackish spots; dorsal rays IX,25-27. To 18 inches (46 cm). Hawai'i and Line Islands to East Africa.

WHITESPOTTED SURGEONFISH   'api   *Acanthurus guttatus* Forster & Schneider, 1801
Brown with 3 white bars, the body and dorsal and anal fins posterior to middle white bar with numerous small white spots; pelvic fins yellow; body deep for the genus; dorsal rays IX,27-30. Largest, 11.3 inches (29 cm). Indo-Pacific; lives in surge zone of exposed rocky shores, often in small schools.

WHITEBAR SURGEONFISH   māikoiko   *Acanthurus leucopareius* (Jenkins, 1903)
Gray-brown with faint bluish lines or rows of small blue spots on body; a broad white band from origin of dorsal fin across posterior operculum, bordered on each side by a dark brown band; a white bar usually present at base of caudal fin; dorsal rays IX,25-27. Reaches 10 inches (25 cm). Antiequatorial; Hawai'i to southern Japan in the north, and Easter Island to New Caledonia in the south; may form schools.

GOLDRIM SURGEONFISH   *Acanthurus nigricans* (Linnaeus, 1758)
Black with a white spot below and adjacent to eye; a yellow band at base of dorsal and anal fins which broadens to nearly full height of fins posteriorly; caudal fin whitish with a narrow yellow bar; dorsal rays IX,28-31. Largest, 8.4 inches (21 cm). Islands of the tropical Pacific, including eastern Pacific; rare in Hawaiian Islands; most often seen at the island of Hawai'i. *A. glaucopareius* Cuvier is a synonym.

BROWN SURGEONFISH   **māʻiʻiʻi**   *Acanthurus nigrofuscus* (Forsskål, 1775)
Brown, sometimes suffused with lavender; head and chest with orange-yellow dots; a prominent black spot at rear base of dorsal and anal fins; posterior margin of caudal fin white; caudal fin lunate; dorsal rays IX,24-27. Reaches 8 inches (20 cm). Indo-Pacific; common in the Hawaiian Islands. Spawns in large aggregations. Sometimes misidentified as *Acanthurus elongatus* (Lacepède).

BLUELINED SURGEONFISH   maiko   *Acanthurus nigroris* Valenciennes, 1835
Dark brown with irregular longitudinal blue lines on body; a black spot at rear base of dorsal and anal fins (not as large as those of *A. nigrofuscus*); caudal fin with a narrow white posterior margin; caudal fin emarginate; dorsal rays IX,24-27. Islands of Oceania. Attains 10 inches (25 cm).

ORANGEBAND SURGEONFISH

na'ena'e

Acanthurus olivaceus Forster & Schneider, 1801

Grayish brown with a horizontal orange band, broadly edged in deep blue, extending posteriorly from upper end of gill opening; an orange line at base of dorsal fin; a large crescentic white area posteriorly in caudal fin; one color phase (shown above) with head and anterior half of body abruptly paler than posterior body; small juveniles

⇧ **Juvenile**

usually bright yellow; larger juveniles develop the orange band in shoulder region; dorsal rays IX,23-25. Attains 12 inches (30 cm). Islands of Oceania to western Pacific; usually seen over sand substrata near reefs, sometimes in small groups. The stomach of this and related species of the genus is thick-walled and gizzard-like.

THOMPSON'S SURGEONFISH   *Acanthurus thompsoni* (Fowler, 1923)
Dark brown, but capable of rapidly changing to light bluish gray; a black spot at axil of pectoral fins and a short distance below; a small black spot at rear base of dorsal fin; body moderately elongate for the genus; snout short; dorsal rays IX,23-26. Largest, 10.6 inches (27 cm). Indo-Pacific (caudal fin white in non-Hawaiian areas). Feeds on zooplankton well above the bottom.

CONVICT SURGEONFISH   manini   *Acanthurus triostegus* (Linnaeus, 1758)
Greenish white with 6 narrow black bars; dorsal rays IX,22-26; caudal spine small. Largest, from Midway, 10.3 inches (26 cm). Indo-Pacific and tropical eastern Pacific; abundant in Hawai'i where regarded as a subspecies, *A. t. sandvicensis*. Feeds on benthic algae, often in aggregations. Postlarvae seek tidepools where they transform in 4-5 days to juveniles at a length of about 1.25 inches (3.2 cm).

YELLOWFIN SURGEONFISH **pualu** *Acanthurus xanthopterus* Valenciennes, 1835
Purplish gray with or without very irregular longitudinal banding; dorsal and anal fins brownish yellow with 3 or 4 blue bands; outer third of pectoral fins yellow; dorsal rays IX,25-27. Largest of the genus; reaches 22 inches (56 cm). Indo-Pacific and tropical eastern Pacific. Often ranges over sand far from shelter of reef, occasionally in small schools.

BLACK SURGEONFISH

Ctenochaetus hawaiiensis Randall, 1955

Dark olive brown with fine lengthwise yellowish gray lines (underwater from a distance, the fish appears black); juveniles orange with dark gray-blue chevron-like markings (called Chevron Tang in the aquarium trade); dorsal rays VIII,27-29; caudal fin slightly emarginate. Attains 11 inches (28 cm). Islands of Oceania; juveniles generally in coral at depths greater than 50 feet (15 m); adults range into shallower water.

⇑ Juvenile

GOLDRING SURGEONFISH **kole** *Ctenochaetus strigosus* (Bennett, 1828)
Brown with numerous light blue longitudinal lines which extend diagonally into soft part of dorsal and anal fins; a distinct yellow ring around eye; faint blue dots on head; juveniles yellow to yellowish brown; dorsal rays VIII,25-28; caudal fin moderately emarginate. Largest in Hawai'i, 7.2 inches (18.3 cm). Indo-Pacific, but with population differences over the range; common in Hawaiian Islands.

WHITEMARGIN UNICORNFISH *Naso annulatus* (Quoy & Gaimard, 1825)
Dark brown to pale bluish gray; margin of median fins white, edge of lips broadly white, the caudal-fin membranes of large adults also white; juveniles with a white ring around caudal peduncle; adults with a long slender bony horn in front of eye; males with a filament from each corner of caudal fin; dorsal rays V-VI,28-29. To about 3 feet (92 cm). Indo-Pacific; rare in Hawai'i. Adults generally in more than 100 feet (30.5 m); often in small aggregations. *Naso herrei* Smith is a synonym.

PALETAIL UNICORNFISH   **kala lōlō**   *Naso brevirostris* (Valenciennes, 1835)
Brownish to bluish gray; body of adults with vertical dark brown lines and small dark spots dorsally and ventrally; caudal fin whitish except basally; one color phase with anterior fourth of body abruptly pale; a long broad-based tapering horn anterior to eye; caudal fin truncate to slightly rounded; dorsal rays V-VI,27-29. Reported to 2 feet (60 cm). Indo-Pacific. Juveniles and short-horned subadults feed on algae, adults chiefly on zooplankton (their long horn makes grazing on benthic algae very difficult).

GRAY UNICORNFISH   *Naso caesius* Randall & Bell, 1992
Bluish gray to dark brown; when gray, able to quickly assume a pattern of vertically elongate blotches which may be either darker or lighter than ground color; preopercle and operculum without dark borders; caudal fin uniform bluish; no rostral horn; dorsal rays VI-VII,27-30; caudal spines blade-like but not pointed and antrorse. Reaches about 2 feet (60 cm). Islands of Oceania; often seen in small schools, sometimes in association with *N. hexacanthus*.

Sleek Unicornfish. See description on the next page.

SLEEK UNICORNFISH   **kala lōlō, 'ōpelu kala**   *Naso hexacanthus* (Bleeker, 1855)
Brownish gray, shading ventrally to yellowish; edge of operculum and preopercle dark brown; caudal fin blue with a broad posterior yellowish brown margin; can change to dark brown or pale blue; tongue of adults black; no rostral horn; dorsal rays V-VII (rarely V),26-29; caudal spines of large adults pointed and antrorse. Attains about 30 inches (76 cm). Indo-Pacific; not common in less than about 50 feet (15 m); submarine observations to 750 feet (229 m). Often occurs in schools off escarpments.

ORANGESPINE UNICORNFISH   **umaumalei**   *Naso lituratus* (Forster & Schneider, 1801)
Grayish brown with a curved yellow band from corner of mouth to eye; snout in front of band black; lips orange; caudal spines and a broad area around each bright orange; no rostral horn; adult males with a filament from each corner of caudal fin. Reported to 18 inches (46 cm). Indo-Pacific; in the Indian Ocean the dorsal fin is mainly yellow. A popular aquarium fish as a juvenile or subadult.

SPOTTED UNICORNFISH   *Naso maculatus* Randall & Struhsaker, 1981
Gray-brown to bluish gray with numerous small dark brown spots and irregular short lines on body; a nearly continuous dark brown line following lateral line; no rostral horn; blade of caudal spines semicircular; dorsal rays VI-VII,26-28. Reaches 22 inches (55 cm). Known to date only from Hawaiian Islands, southern Japan, and Lord Howe Island. Occurs in as little as 80 feet (24 m) in the Northwestern Hawaiian Islands, but below the usual diving depths in the main islands.

BLUESPINE UNICORNFISH   **kala**   *Naso unicornis* (Forsskål, 1775)
Light olive to yellowish gray; caudal spines and a small area around each bright blue; dorsal and anal fins with oblique dark bands and blue margins; a tapering bony horn in front of eye, not extending anterior to mouth; dorsal profile of snout forming an angle of about 45°; dorsal rays usually VI,27-30. Reaches 27 inches (69 cm). Indo-Pacific; ranges into surprisingly shallow water in search of its algal food.

Yellow Tang. See description on the next page.

YELLOW TANG   lau'ipala

Zebrasoma flavescens (Bennett, 1828)

Bright yellow except for white sheath of caudal spine; snout prominently pointed; dorsal and anal fins high (especially in juveniles); dorsal rays V,23-26. Reaches 8 inches (20 cm). North Pacific from the Hawaiian Islands to southern Japan, but abundant only in Hawai'i. The young tend to hide among branches of finger coral; adults will graze algae near the shore in calm areas. A very popular aquarium fish (more are exported from Hawai'i than any other species). The closely related dark brown non-Hawaiian *Zebrasoma scopas* interbreeds with the Yellow Tang when the latter is rare (as in the Marshall Islands).

⇑ **Juvenile**

SAILFIN TANG   māneoneo   *Zebrasoma veliferum* (Bloch, 1797)
Alternating broad gray-brown bars containing orange lines (except first 2 with orange spots) and narrow white bars containing 1 or 2 yellow lines; caudal fin largely yellow; caudal spine in a blue spot; juveniles with yellow and black bars; dorsal and anal fins extremely high (raised by adults when alarmed; these fins remain elevated in juveniles); dorsal rays IV,29-33. Largest, 15.5 inches (40 cm). Central and western Pacific; a similar species, *Zebrasoma desjardinii* (Bennett), in the Indian Ocean.

BARRACUDAS (SPHYRAENIDAE)

The barracudas (all in the genus *Sphyraena*) are easily recognized by their very elongate and little compressed bodies, large mouth with protruding pointed lower jaw, very large compressed teeth, and 2 widely separated dorsal fins, the first of V spines, and the second of I spine and 9 soft rays. As their awesome dentition would suggest, they are carnivorous, feeding mainly on other fishes. The

Great Barracuda *(Sphyraena barracuda)* has been known to inflict severe wounds on humans, but nearly all the attacks have taken place in murky water where a limb might be mistaken for a fish, or from provocation (as by spearing). In clear water without anything that might be attracting, such as a wounded fish struggling on a spear or a metal object that flashes in the sun, there should be no reason to fear a barracuda. Some species form schools by day and disperse at night to feed. Others such as *S. barracuda* are diurnal and usually solitary. Only two species are positively known from the Hawaiian Islands, but the author recently observed an adult of *S. qenie* Klunzinger near South Point on the Kona coast of Hawai'i.

GREAT BARRACUDA   kākū   *Sphyraena barracuda* (Walbaum, 1792)
Dark gray on back, silvery below; adults usually with a few scattered black spots, mainly on lower posterior half of body; caudal fin with a large black area on upper and lower lobes (also often on second dorsal fin); subadults and juveniles with slightly oblique dark bars on back; lateral-line scales 69-90. Reported to 5.5 feet (1.7 m); world angling record 87 lbs. (38.5 kg). Circumglobal in tropical and subtropical seas. New World fish lack the large black area in the second dorsal and caudal fin lobes. Often implicated in ciguatera poisoning. The young occur in shallow estuarine or mangrove areas.

HELLER'S BARRACUDA   kawele'ā   *Sphyraena helleri* Jenkins, 1901
Silvery with iridescence and 2 brassy stripes on side of body; eye large; lateral-line scales 120-135; a single gill raker (none in *S. barracuda*). Grows to 32 inches (80 cm). Central and western Pacific. Forms large, essentially stationary schools by day; presumed to disperse individually to feed at night.

LEFTEYE FLOUNDERS (BOTHIDAE)

Flatfishes lie on the bottom on one of the sides with both eyes on the upper side. As larvae they are like normal fishes with one eye on each side, but before settling out of the plankton, one eye slowly migrates over the top of the head to the other side. The species of Bothidae, the largest family of flatfishes, have the eyes on the left side (with few exceptions). The eyes may be elevated, and each moves independently of the other. There are no spines in the fins, and the dorsal fin originates above or before the upper eye. The pelvic fins have 6 or fewer rays; the pelvic fin of the blind side is short-based, its origin posterior to the fin of the eyed side. There is a single lateral line on the eyed side, highly arched over the pectoral fin (lateral line of the blind side faint or absent on some species). Males may have one or more spines on the snout, and their eyes may be farther apart than those of females. Most species occur on open sand or mud substrata. They generally match the color of the bottom closely and can change color quickly; also they are able to quickly bury themselves in the sediment. All are carnivorous, usually ambushing their prey of small fishes and crustaceans. Thirteen species occur in the Hawaiian Islands; the two most apt to be encountered inshore are presented below.

FLOWERY FLOUNDER   **pāki'i**   *Bothus mancus* (Broussonet, 1782)
Pale yellowish with numerous small dusky spots, small dark-edged pale blue spots, and large pale blue circles or partial circles containing lesser spots; 2 large midlateral blackish spots; dorsal rays 95-104; anal rays 74-81; eyes of males far apart, and pectoral fin very long (the illustrated fish is a male). Attains 18 inches (46 cm). Indo-Pacific and tropical eastern Pacific; often found within coral reefs. Sometimes called Peacock Flounder, but this common name belongs to an Atlantic flatfish.

PANTHER FLOUNDER   **pāki'i**   *Bothus pantherinus* (Rüppell, 1830)
Color similar to *B. mancus* but usually with numerous small yellow spots, and the blue circles tend to be broken into roseates of small blue spots; dorsal rays 85-95; anal rays 64-72; eyes of males far apart; pectoral fin of eyed side of males very long. To 12 inches (30 cm). Indo-Pacific; occurs on sand or silty sand, sometimes in the vicinity of coral reefs but not within the reef environment.

SLENDER FLOUNDERS (SAMARIDAE)

This family of small slender flatfishes was considered a subfamily of the Pleuronectidae (righteye flounders) until recently. Three genera are known, with a total of about 20 species, most of which occur in deep water. All have the eyes on the right side. Only two species, both in the genus *Samariscus*, are found in Hawaiian waters. *S. corallinus* Gilbert occurs in more than 250 feet (77 m).

THREESPOT FLOUNDER   *Samariscus triocellatus* Woods, 1966
Finely mottled light brown with a longitudinal row of 3 large blackish spots containing yellow centers, the first beneath tip of pectoral fin, the last before lower half of caudal fin; pectoral rays black; dorsal rays 62-70, the first 2 or 3 slightly anterior to eyes; anal rays 47-56; pectoral rays 5 (first very small). Reaches 2.8 inches (7 cm). Indo-Pacific; in coral reefs. Often holds the pectoral fin erect.

SOLES (SOLEIDAE)

This flatfish family is easily characterized by having the eyes on the right side, the edge of the preopercle covered by skin, the mouth curved, the dorsal fin over or anterior to the eyes, and the pelvic fins free from the anal fin; the pectoral fins are absent on some species; the lateral line is straight on the body. Soles often bury in the sediment of the bottom. Some remain hidden in sand or mud by day, emerging to forage at night. The species of *Pardachirus* and at least some of *Aseraggodes* are known to produce a strong skin toxin when under stress. Two species are known from the Hawaiian Islands, both in the genus *Aseraggodes*.

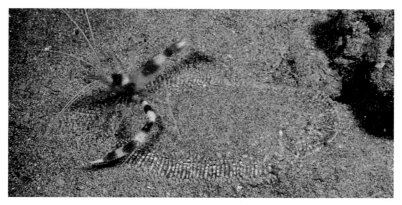

BOREHAM'S SOLE   *Aseraggodes borehami* Randall 1996
Light brown, blotched with brown spots of variable size and numerous small irregular white blotches, the most white at upper end of gill opening; dorsal rays 71-75; anal rays 49-52; no pectoral fins; lateral-line scales 68-72; front of upper lip not overlapping lower lip when mouth closed.. Largest, 5.3 inches (13.4 cm). Hawaiian Islands. Often found in sand on the floor of caves or beneath ledges. The illustrated individual is being cleaned by the banded coral shrimp, *Stenopus hispidus*, one claw of which is missing.

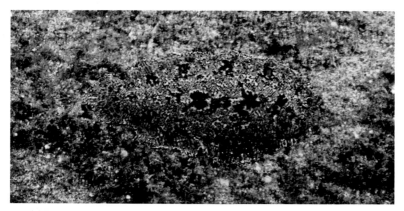

Therese's Sole. See description on the next page.

THERESE'S SOLE *Aseraggodes therese* Randall, 1996
Brown, mottled with white, with three longitudinal rows of large, irregular dark brown blotches and a few scattered lesser dark blotches; dorsal rays 72-79; anal rays 54-61; lateral-line scales 60-66; front of upper lip overlapping lower lip when mouth closed. A small species, the largest, 3 inches (7.7 cm). Known only from the Hawaiian Islands; usually found by day buried in silty sand in caves. Formerly misidentified as *A. kobensis* (Steindachner), a Japanese species.

TRIGGERFISHES (BALISTIDAE)

Triggerfishes are named for the mechanism whereby the first dorsal spine can be locked in erect position by the small second spine; if one presses down on the second dorsal spine (the trigger), the first spine can be moved. These fishes are deep-bodied with the eye high on the head, a long snout, and small mouth. The teeth in the jaws are close-set and chisel-like, the upper jaw with 8 in an outer row and 6 in an inner row which serves to buttress the outer; the gill opening is a short slit anterior to the upper part of the pectoral fin; the skin is tough and rough to touch, the scales nonoverlapping. Some species have small, forward-curved spines posteriorly on the side of the body. There are 2 dorsal fins, the first of III spines; there are no pelvic fins. Triggerfishes are usually solitary except when they form pairs at spawning time. A notable exception is the Black Durgon (*Melichthys niger*) which may form aggregations.

Balistid fishes normally swim by undulating the second dorsal and anal fins, using their tail only for rapid movement. When frightened, they may take refuge in a hole in the reef into which they can barely pass; they then erect their first dorsal spine and extend their pelvic bone to wedge themselves in position. At night they enter the same or similar hole to sleep. Most feed on invertebrates with hard skel-etal parts such as crabs, mol-lusks, and sea urchins; they readily reduce such prey to pieces with their powerful jaws and sharp teeth. The spe-

Aggregation of Black Durgon (*Melichthys niger*).

cies of the genera *Melichthys* and *Xanthichthys* feed heavily on zooplankton. Triggerfishes, in general, are not good aquarium fishes because they may attack other fishes in the tank. Also they soon consume any resident crustaceans.

The pelagic juvenile stage of the species of *Melichthys* reaches surprisingly large size, to more than 6 inches (15 cm). The transforming stage of the Pinktail Durgon (*Melichthys vidua*) was twice described as a new species in different genera, *Pachynathus nycteris* Jordan & Evermann and *Oncobalistes erythropterus* Fowler.

Triggerfishes lay demersal eggs which are aggressively guarded by the female parent. Two of the largest species have bitten divers (including the author) who made the mistake of venturing too close to the nest. These species are the Titan Triggerfish (*Balistoides viridescens*) and the Yellowspotted Triggerfish (*Pseudobalistes fuscus*); they occur throughout most of the Indo-Pacific region, but not the Hawaiian Islands. The guarding females of Hawaiian species sometimes threaten by swimming aggressively toward an intruder, and they have the capability of inflicting a bite.

Triggerfishes are well known for making a grunting noise. This is produced by intercostal muscles moving two bones in the pectoral girdle; the swimbladder then serves as a resonating chamber for the sound.

Eleven species are known from the Hawaiian Islands, nine of which are discussed below. Not included are *Canthidermis maculatus* (Bloch), which is pelagic (hence not often seen, except when it comes inshore for spawning and prepares a shallow crater on sand bottom for the nest) and *Xanthichthys caeruleolineatus* Randall, Matsuura & Zama, which is rare in Hawaii and found only in deep water (the Hawaiian record will be reported by the author and Bruce C. Mundy). The general Hawaiian name for triggerfishes is **humuhumu**.

FINESCALE TRIGGERFISH   *Balistes polylepis* Steindachner, 1876
Light olive brown to bluish gray, without any distinctive markings; dorsal soft rays 26-28; third dorsal spine nearly as long as second; soft dorsal and anal fins strongly elevated anteriorly, and caudal fin with pointed lobes; no grooves on cheek; no ridges or tubercles posteriorly on body. Reported to 30 inches (76 cm). California to Chile; rare in Hawai'i where it may only be a stray from the eastern Pacific.

BLACK DURGON **humuhumu 'ele'ele** *Melichthys niger* (Bloch, 1786)
Dark gray to dark blue-green with black longitudinal lines following scale rows; a narrow pale blue band at base of soft dorsal and anal fins; often displays bright blue lines from eye across top of head; dorsal soft rays 30-34; longitudinal ridges following scale rows posteriorly on body. Largest, 12.5 inches (32 cm), from Laysan. Circumtropical; when common, may form aggregations. Very abundant at Johnston Island. Feeds mainly on algae (about 70% of diet) and zooplankton.

PINKTAIL DURGON **humuhumu hi'ukole** *Melichthys vidua* (Solander, 1844)
Dark brown to nearly black, often with a yellowish cast; scaled basal part of caudal fin white, remaining fin pink; second dorsal and anal fins whitish with a black border; dorsal soft rays 31-35; slight longitudinal ridges following scales posteriorly on body. Largest, 13.4 inches (34 cm). Indo-Pacific; feeds mainly on algae and detritus, occasionally on crustaceans, octopuses, sponges, and fishes.

LAGOON TRIGGERFISH   humuhumu nukunuku apua'a
Rhinecanthus aculeatus (Linnaeus, 1758)
Pale greenish gray, shading to white below, with a large blackish area on body with radiating bands; blue
and black lines across interorbital; a long orange-yellow streak extending from mouth; rows of black
antrorse spines posteriorly on side of body; dorsal rays 23-26. Reaches 12 inches (30 cm). Indo-Pacific
and eastern south Atlantic; not common in Hawai'i. Prefers shallow protected waters. Feeds on algae and
invertebrates, including mollusks, crustaceans, polychaete worms, and heart urchins.

REEF TRIGGERFISH   humuhumu nukunuku apua'a
Rhinecanthus rectangulus (Bloch & Schneider, 1801)
Light brown, shading to white below, with an oblique black band extending below eye and broadening
on body; a gold-bordered black triangle containing antrorse spines posteriorly on body, preceded by a
parallel gold line; blue and black lines across interorbital; a red bar at pectoral base; dorsal rays 22-25. To
10 inches (25 cm). Indo-Pacific; inshore on reefs. Feeds mainly on algae and small benthic invertebrates.

LEI TRIGGERFISH

humuhumu lei

Sufflamen bursa (Bloch & Schneider, 1801)

Grayish brown, whitish below a white line from mouth to anal-fin origin, with a scimitar-shaped dark brown to yellow bar through eye, and a second bar posterior to it; dorsal soft rays 27-30. Attains 8.5 inches (21.5 cm). Indo-Pacific; common in Hawai'i. Feeds on algae, crabs and other crustaceans, mollusks, sea urchins, worms, eggs, and tunicates.

⇡ **Juvenile**

BRIDLED TRIGGERFISH **humuhumu mimi** *Sufflamen fraenatus* (Latreille, 1804)
Grayish brown, often with a broad whitish bar at base of caudal fin; a yellow line at base of lower lip; males with a narrow pink to yellow band under chin, linking with a narrow pale band extending from mouth across lower head; dorsal soft rays 28-31. Reported to 15 inches (38 cm). Indo-Pacific. Feeds mainly on sea urchins, fishes, mollusks, tunicates, brittle stars, crustaceans, worms, and sponges.

Male ⇑   ⇓ Female

GILDED TRIGGERFISH   *Xanthichthys auromarginatus* (Bennett, 1831)
Brownish gray with a bluish or lavender cast, the scales with a small whitish spot (most evident ventrally); margins of median fins yellow on males and dark reddish brown on females; males with a large blue patch on lower part of head; dorsal rays 27-30; grooves separating scale rows on head; ridges posteriorly on body. Largest, 7.7 inches (19.5 cm). Indo-Pacific. Feeds on zooplankton.

Male ⇑   ⇓ Female

CROSSHATCH TRIGGERFISH *Xanthichthys mento* (Jordan & Gilbert, 1882)
Brownish yellow, the scales rimmed with dark brown (hence a crosshatch pattern); blue lines following grooves on head; males with a blue spot on each scale, a red caudal fin, and yellow edges on soft dorsal and anal fins; females with a yellow-edged caudal fin and reddish borders on soft dorsal and anal fins; dorsal rays 28-32. Reaches 12 inches (30 cm). Antitropical in the Pacific; records include Japan, southern California, Easter Island, and Pitcairn Island. Common in diving depths in the Northwestern Hawaiian Islands; usually deeper than normal diving depths in the main islands. Feeds on zooplankton.

FILEFISHES (MONACANTHIDAE)

The filefishes are named for their tough, finely abrasive skin. They share many features with the triggerfishes, differing in their more compressed bodies, generally a more pointed snout, a more slender and longer first dorsal spine (also capable of being locked in erect position), a very small second dorsal spine (absent in a few species), and no third dorsal spine. The dentition is similar but there are 6 teeth in the outer row of the upper jaw and 4 in the inner. The scales have numerous tiny setae which obscure the scale outlines. Unlike the triggerfishes, many species are able to alter their color to match their surroundings; also many have little cutaneous flaps or cirri that further enhance their camouflage. Because of this and their secretive nature, they are easily overlooked. Some filefishes are sexually dimorphic, especially with respect to the spines or setae posteriorly on the body (larger in males).

The fishes of this family are mostly omnivorous, feeding on a wide variety of benthic plant and animal life. Some filefishes, such as *Aluterus scriptus,* ingest noxious sponges and various stinging coelenterates avoided by other fishes. Eight species occur in the Hawaiian Islands, one of which, *Thamnaconus garretti* (Fowler), is restricted to deep water.

There are more species of filefishes in Australia (where they are known as leatherjackets) than anywhere in the world; they occur along all the coasts of the continent, including the cool southern shore where a surprising 23 species are recorded.

UNICORN FILEFISH — *Aluterus monoceros* (Linnaeus, 1758)
Light gray to brown, often faintly dark mottled and spotted; dorsal profile of head slightly convex, the ventral profile initially concave; eye an eye diameter or more below dorsal profile of head; first dorsal spine long and slender, above eye; soft dorsal rays 45-51; caudal fin of adults short and truncate to emarginate. Attains 30 inches (76 cm). Worldwide in tropical and subtropical seas; rare in Hawai'i.

SCRAWLED FILEFISH   loulu   *Aluterus scriptus* (Osbeck, 1765)
Light bluish gray to olive-brown with blue or blue-green spots and short irregular bands and scattered small black spots; dorsal and ventral profiles of head concave; eye about a half eye diameter from top of head; first dorsal spine long and slender, over eye; soft dorsal rays 43-49; caudal fin very long and rounded. Reaches 30 inches (76 cm). Cosmopolitan in all warm seas. Feeds on algae, gorgonians, stinging coral and other noxious coelenterates, tunicates, and sponges.

Male Barred Filefish. See description on the next page.

Female Barred Filefish. See description on the next page.

BARRED FILEFISH **'ō'ili** *Cantherhines dumerilii* (Hollard, 1854).
Grayish brown with indistinct dark brown bars posteriorly on side of body; a pink to whitish submarginal band on lips; males with caudal fin, the 2 pairs of peduncular spines, and a large spot in front of each anterior spine orange; juveniles may be white-spotted; dorsal soft rays 34-39. Attains 15 inches (38 cm). Indo-Pacific and tropical eastern Pacific; often in pairs. Feeds mainly on branching corals, but other invertebrates are also eaten. *C. carolae* (Jordan & McGregor) and *C. albopunctatus* (Seale) are synonyms.

SQUARETAIL FILEFISH **'ō'ili lepa** *Cantherhines sandwichiensis* (Quoy & Gaimard, 1824)
Brown to gray, sometimes with indistinct small pale spots; a white spot at rear base of soft dorsal fin; dorsal, anal, and pectoral rays usually yellow; caudal fin truncate to slightly rounded; soft dorsal rays 33-36. Largest, 7.6 inches (19.4 cm). Hawaiian Islands; closely related to *C. pardalis* from elsewhere in the Indo-Pacific, and *C. pullus* from the tropical and subtropical Atlantic. Feeds mainly on algae and detritus, but also ingests tunicates, corals, sponges and other benthic animals.

SHY FILEFISH **'ō'ili** *Cantherhines verecundus* (E. K. Jordan, 1925)
Light gray to olive brown with small dark blotches arranged mainly in longitudinal rows on body; able to darken to a strongly mottled pattern; juveniles may be green; caudal fin rounded; soft dorsal rays 34-36; skin with numerous small cirri. Largest, 6.3 inches (16 cm). Hawaiian Islands; not common.

YELLOWTAIL FILEFISH   'ō'ili   *Pervagor aspricaudus* (Hollard, 1854)
Brown, often shading posteriorly to orange-yellow; caudal fin yellow with orange cross lines on rays and a black posterior border containing irregular yellow lines and spots; soft dorsal and anal fins yellow with blue dots forming lines; dorsal soft rays 31-35. Largest, 4.7 inches (12 cm). Antiequatorial in the Indo-Pacific. Not common and very shy.

FANTAIL FILEFISH   'ō'ili 'uwi'uwi   *Pervagor spilosoma* (Lay & Bennett, 1839)
Yellow to yellowish brown, the body with numerous close-set dark brown spots, the head with oblique dark brown lines; caudal fin orange to red with a yellow posterior margin and broad black submarginal band; dorsal soft rays 37-39. Largest, 7.1 inches (18 cm). Hawaiian Islands. Varies in abundance; in some years occurs in enormous numbers, with dead specimens washing ashore on beaches. Feeds on algae, detritus, and a wide variety of benthic invertebrates.

TRUNKFISHES (OSTRACIIDAE)

The trunkfishes, also popularly known as boxfishes, are unique in possessing a bony carapace of polygonal plates with gaps for the mouth, gill opening, caudal peduncle, and fins. The carapace may be triangular, quadrangular, pentagonal, hexagonal, or nearly round in cross-section; its surface is usually rough due to small tubercles on the plates. Some of the species have stout spines which project from the carapace. The mouth is small and low on the head; the gill opening is a short near-vertical slit. There are no spines in the fins;

the dorsal and anal fins are posterior in position, usually with 9 rays; there are no pelvic fins. As would be expected from their bony armor and boxy shape, trunkfishes are slow swimmers; the usual progression is by a sculling action of the dorsal and anal fins; the caudal fin is brought into play when the fishes want to move faster. They feed on a wide variety of benthic animals, especially sessile forms such as tunicates and sponges; many also ingest large amounts of algae. Some trunkfishes, at least, secrete a skin toxin when under stress. Six species are recorded from the Hawaiian Islands; one of these occurs only in deep water. Another, *Ostracion cubicus*, is known from Hawai'i from only one specimen and one sighting.

SPINY COWFISH   *Lactoria diaphana* (Bloch & Schneider, 1801)
Yellowish gray to light brown, shading to pale yellow or white ventrally, with scattered dark blotches and small dark spots on back and sides; carapace of 5 ridges, the median one on back with a large compressed spine; ridge along upper side with a small lateral spine, ending in a forward-directed spine above eye; lower ridge ending posteriorly in a spine; ventral surface of carapace broadly convex. Reaches 10 inches (25 cm). Indo-Pacific and tropical eastern Pacific; rare in Hawai'i.

THORNBACK COWFISH   **makukana**   *Lactoria fornasini* (Bianconi, 1846)
Light yellowish brown with large diffuse dusky blotches and scattered light blue spots and short lines; joints of carapace plates dark brown; carapace and spines as described for *L. diaphana*, but without a lateral spine on upper ridge. Largest examined, 5.5 inches (14 cm). Indo-Pacific, but not recorded from many localities; occurs more on sand and rubble bottoms than on coral reefs.

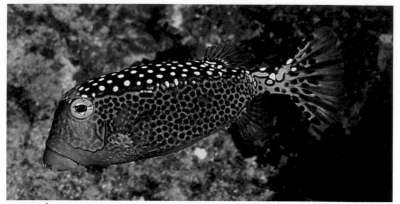

Male ⇑   ⇓ Female

SPOTTED BOXFISH **moa** *Ostracion meleagris* (Shaw & Nodder, 1796)
Males blue on side with numerous small black spots; upper surface of carapace brown with white spots; some orange spots along upper caudal peduncle, dorsal ridge, and eye; females brown with small white spots; carapace quadrangular, the sides concave, the upper and lower surfaces convex. Largest, 6.2 inches (15.7 cm). Indo-Pacific; subspecifically different in Hawai'i, *Ostracion meleagris camurum* Jenkins.

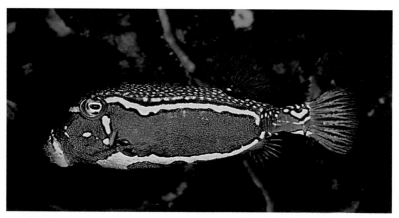

Male Whitley's Trunkfish. See description on the next page.

Female ⇑

WHITLEY'S TRUNKFISH   moa   *Ostracion whitleyi* Fowler, 1931
Males dark grayish blue with white spots on the back and an irregular black-edged white stripe along the ridges, the upper continuing across head in front of eyes; females yellowish brown with small white spots to level of lower edge of eye; a broad white stripe on side; carapace similar to that of *O. meleagris*, but the ridges sharper, and there is a low ridge ventrally at front of carapace. Largest, 6.3 inches (16 cm). Hawaiian Islands to French Polynesia; rare in Hawai'i, especially the male form.

PUFFERS (TETRAODONTIDAE)

The puffers are named for their ability, when alarmed, to enlarge their bodies by drawing water (or air if out of the sea) into a highly distensible ventral diverticulum of the stomach. They are characterized further by having the teeth in their jaws fused to beak-like dental plates (with a median suture); a slit-like gill opening in front of pectoral-fin base; dorsal and anal fins posterior in position, without spines; no pelvic fins; and no ribs. The skin is tough and without scales, but small spinules are often present, especially ventrally. Puffers are well known for producing a powerful poison, tetradotoxin, in their tissues, especially the liver and ovaries. The toxin varies greatly in strength in the different species, some being safe to eat, and others potentially lethal; it can also vary with geographical area and the reproductive season. Most puffers are solitary but a few form small aggregations.

Fourteen species of puffers are recorded from Hawaii. The nine species most often encountered inshore in Hawaiian waters are presented below. Not included are *Arothron manilensis* (Procé) and *Canthigaster solandri* (Richardson) which are known from only one and two specimens respectively, hence probably waifs; and *Canthigaster inframacula* Randall and Struhsaker, *Lagocephalus lagocephalus* (Linnaeus), and *Sphoeroides pachygaster* (Müller & Troschel) which are pelagic or known only from deep water.

STRIPEBELLY PUFFER **o'opu hue** *Arothron hispidus* (Linnaeus, 1758)
Olive to gray dorsally with scattered small white spots, shading to white on sides and ventrally; a black area with white circles around pectoral-fin base; dark stripes usually present on abdomen; dorsal and anal rays 10 or 11. Largest, 19 inches (48.5 cm). Indo-Pacific and tropical eastern Pacific; occurs from estuaries to coral reefs. Feeds on algae and a wide variety of benthic invertebrates.

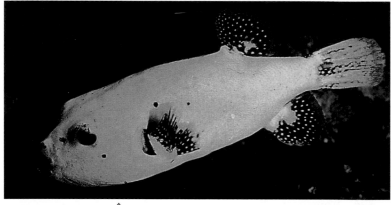

Yellow Color Phase ⇑   ⇓ **Normal Color Phase**

Spotted Puffer. See description on the next page.

SPOTTED PUFFER **o'opu hue** *Arothron meleagris* (Bloch & Schneider, 1801)
Brown to nearly black with small white spots; one rare color phase entirely bright yellow; dorsal rays 11 or 12; anal rays 12 or 13. Largest examined, 13.5 inches (34 cm). Indo-Pacific and tropical eastern Pacific. A coral-reef species; feeds mainly on corals, but also ingests sponges, mollusks, bryozoans, tunicates, polychaete worms, algae, and detritus.

AMBON TOBY *Canthigaster amboinensis* (Bleeker, 1865)
Olivaceous to light brown with small light blue spots on body, except ventrally, and small dark brown spots and short irregular lines; blue lines radiating from eye; head brownish yellow with small blue spots and lines; dorsal rays usually 12; anal rays usually 11. Largest, 5.2 inches (13.2 cm). Indo-Pacific and Galapagos Islands; occurs in shallow reef and rocky shore areas exposed to surge.

CROWN TOBY *Canthigaster coronata* (Vaillant & Sauvage, 1875)
White with scattered yellow dots, a black band across interorbital, and 3 black bars on body that are broader dorsally (the first vertical, the second slightly oblique, and the third very oblique); yellow and blue lines radiating from eye; dorsal and anal rays usually 9 or 10. Largest, 5.3 inches (13.5 cm). Indo-Pacific; usually found on sand or rubble bottoms at depths greater than about 65 feet (20 m).

LANTERN TOBY   *Canthigaster epilampra* (Jenkins, 1903)
Olive brown dorsally, shading to white ventrally on body and yellowish on head, with small blue spots and lines (the lines radiating from eye bright blue); a large dark brown spot at base of dorsal fin and extending diagonally downward and forward; caudal fin yellow; dorsal rays 10; anal rays usually 9. Largest, 4.3 inches (11 cm). Central and western Pacific, generally at depths greater than 80 feet (24.5 m). Often found in the vicinity of caves.

HAWAIIAN WHITESPOTTED TOBY   *Canthigaster jactator* (Jenkins, 1901)
Yellowish brown to dark brown with numerous close-set white to pale blue spots on head and body; no spots on fins; dorsal and anal rays 8-10. Largest, 3.5 inches (8.9 cm). Hawaiian Islands; a very common shallow-water reef fish. Stomach contents of 22 specimens: sponges (37.5%), algae and detritus (22%), tunicates (13.5%), and other benthic invertebrates.

MAZE TOBY   *Canthigaster rivulata* (Temminck & Schlegel, 1850)
Two irregular brown stripes containing yellow dots on side of body, linked around front of gill opening,
the upper broader and darker; body above upper stripe yellow with blue dots and irregular lines; body
below stripes white with faint blue dots and lines; a dark brown spot below dorsal fin; dorsal and anal
rays usually 10. Largest, 7.7 inches (19.5 cm). Indo-Pacific; not common in Hawai'i. Usually found in more
than 100 feet (30.5 m); deepest, 1170 feet (357 m).

FLORAL PUFFER   *Torquigener florealis* (Cope, 1871)
White with a row of orange-yellow spots extending posteriorly from upper end of gill opening; body and
postorbital head above spots with brown dots outlining numerous small oval white spots; caudal fin
truncate; dorsal rays usually 10; anal rays usually 8. Largest, 7.3 inches (18.5 cm). Hawai'i to Japan and
East China Sea; usually over sand. Varies greatly in abundance from year to year.

RANDALL'S PUFFER   *Torquigener randalli* Hardy, 1983
An irregular dark brown stripe (which may contain orange spots) from above gill opening to base of
caudal fin; back above stripe gray with numerous dark brown dots and small white spots; body below
stripe white; 3 blackish blotches on side of head, the largest below eye; caudal fin truncate; dorsal rays 8
or 9; anal rays 7 or 8; reaches about 5 inches (12.7 cm). Hawaiian Islands, over sand. Known from depths
of 50 to at least 330 feet (15-100 m).

PORCUPINEFISHES (DIODONTIDAE)

The fishes of this family are similar in many respects to the puffers, such as the ability to inflate themselves, having a short gill opening in front of the pectoral fin, no spines in fins, and no pelvic fins. They differ notably in having prominent spines which cover much of the head and body. The spines may be 3-rooted, hence fixed (as seen on *Chilomycterus*), or 2-rooted and movable (as on *Diodon*). Normally, the spines of *Diodon* lie against the side of the body, but when the fishes inflate themselves they are erected to nearly right angles (therefore a deterrent to most predators). Porcupinefishes dif-

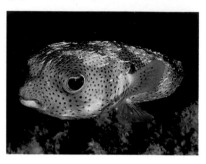

fer further from puffers in lacking a median suture to their dental plates, having larger eyes, and broader pectoral fins (often with posterior edge emarginate). Diodontid fishes appear to be nocturnal. Their powerful jaws and beak-like dental plates are well suited to crush the hard tests of sea urchins, the shells of mollusks and hermit crabs, and the exoskeletons of crabs.

SPOTTED BURRFISH   *Chilomycterus reticulatus* (Linnaeus, 1758)
Light gray to light brown dorsally, white below, with scattered black spots on head and body, 2 broad dusky bars on head (one beneath eye) and 2 on body, and numerous small black spots on fins; spines on head and body short and immovable; dorsal rays 12-14; anal rays 11-14. Reaches 21.5 inches (55 cm). Circumglobal in subtropical to warm temperate seas; rare in Hawai'i.

SPINY BALLOONFISH **kōkala** *Diodon holocanthus* Linnaeus, 1758
Light olive to light brown, shading to white ventrally, with scattered small black spots; a dark brown bar through eye, a transverse dark bar on top of head, another dorsally in middle of body, a large dark brown spot above pectoral fin, and one around base of dorsal fin; fins usually without spots; 2 small barbels on chin; spines dorsally on head longer than those behind pectoral fins. Attains 15 inches (38 cm). Circumglobal; more common in subtropical than tropical localities.

PORCUPINEFISH **kōkala** *Diodon hystrix* Linnaeus, 1758.
Olive to light gray-brown dorsally with numerous small black spots, white ventrally; fins with numerous small black spots; head very large; no barbels on chin; spines posterior to pectoral fins longer than those dorsally on head. Reaches 28 inches (72 cm). Circumtropical, mainly on coral reefs. Feeds principally on mollusks (especially gastropods), sea urchins, crabs, and hermit crabs.

GLOSSARY

Adipose fin: a small fleshy fin without rays found on the back behind the dorsal fin of some primitive teleost fishes such as lizardfishes.

Anal fin: the fin along the ventral part of the body supported by rays in bony fishes; usually commences just behind the anus (vent).

Antipatharian: pertaining to an order of benthic marine animals of the Class Anthozoa, Phylum Coelenterata; commonly called black corals.

Antrorse: directed forward, as in reference to the direction of a spine; the opposite of retrorse.

Bar: an elongate, vertical, straight-sided, color marking.

Barbel: a slender, tentacle-like protuberance of sensory function often seen on the chin of some fishes such as goatfishes.

Benthic: referring to the benthos, the fauna and flora of the sea bottom.

Branchiostegal rays: slender bones ventrally on the head which support the gill membranes.

Bryozoan: an aquatic, plant-like or encrusting animals of the Phylum Bryozoa, commonly called moss animals; they are sessile, colonial, with a complete digestive tract and ciliated tentacles around the mouth.

Canine: a prominent, slender, sharp-pointed tooth.

Carapace: a rigid bony shield encasing the body or part of it.

Carnivore: a flesh-eating animal.

Caudal fin: tail fin; the term tail alone properly refers to that part of a fish posterior to the anus.

Caudal peduncle: the part of the body of a fish between the posterior base of the anal fin and the base of the caudal fin.

Cephalic: referring to the head.

Ciguatera: an illness from eating a fresh fish (even when fully cooked) which has ciguatoxin in its tissues. The toxin is produced by a benthic dinoflagellate which is eaten incidentally by algal-feeding fishes and invertebrates and passed on to carnivorous fishes that accumulate the toxin to dangerous levels.

Coelenterate: an aquatic animal of the Phylum Coelenterata; characterized by a mouth surrounded by tentacles bearing nematocysts (stinging cells) and lacking an anus; includes sea anemones, corals, and jellyfishes.

Commensal: refers to an association of two different organisms whereby one gains benefit by living with, on, or within another, but without harm or benefit to the other.

Community: an assemblage of animals and plants living together in one habitat.

Compressed: laterally flattened; often used in reference to the shape of the body of a fish - in this case clearly narrower than deep.

Copepod: a small to microscopic aquatic animal of the Subclass Copepoda, Class Crustacea; may be free-living (benthic or pelagic), commensal, or parasitic. A major component of the zooplankton.

Crustacean: an animal of the Class Crustacea, Phylum Arthropoda; includes crabs, lobsters, shrimps, and copepods.

Cryptic: in reference to animal that tends to remain hidden.

Ctenoid scales: scales of bony fishes with tiny tooth-like projections along the posterior margin and exposed part of the scales. Collectively these little teeth (called cteni) impart a rough texture to the surface of the scales.

Cycloid scales: scales of bony fishes, the edges and exposed part of which are smooth.

Demersal: living on the sea bottom.

Depth: when used in reference to the structure of a fish, it means the maximum height of the body excluding the fins.

Distal: outward from the point of attachment; the opposite of proximal.

Dorsal fin: the median fin along the back which is supported by rays.

Echinoid: referring to the Class Echinoidea of the Phylum Echinodermata; includes the sea urchins and sand dollars.

Ectoparasite: a parasite living on the external part of an animal or within the gill chamber.

Emarginate: concave; used to describe the shape of the posterior border of a caudal fin which is inwardly curved.

Endemic: native; in reference to an animal or plant restricted to an area such as an island or group of islands.

Euryhaline: tolerant of a wide range of salinity.

Eurythermal: tolerant of a wide range of temperature.

Falcate: sickle-shape; often used to describe the shape of fins.

Family: a major entity in the classification of animals and plants consisting of a group of related genera. Family words end in idae. If used as an adjective, the ae is dropped, thus Gobiidae as an adjective becomes gobiid. Related families group to form orders.

Finlet: a small median fin, usually occurring in a series, posterior to the second dorsal and anal fins of scombrid fishes (tunas and mackerels) and in some carangid fishes (jacks).

Foraminifera: an order of single-cell animals of the Phylum Protozoa, mostly tiny, which are covered by a shell; they may be benthic, pelagic, or commensal.

Forked: inwardly angular, used in describing the shape of a caudal fin which is divided into 2 equal lobes, the posterior margin of which is relatively straight.

Genus: a group of related species. The first word of a scientific name (always capitalized).

Gill arch: The bony and cartilaginous support for the gill filaments (where the gaseous exchange of respiration takes place). Normally there are four pairs of gill arches in bony fishes.

Gill opening: The opening posteriorly (and often ventrally as well) on the head where the water of respiration is expelled. Bony fishes have a single gill opening whereas cartilaginous fishes (sharks and rays) have five to seven; the gill openings of sharks and rays are usually called gill slits.

Gill rakers: stout protuberances of the gill arch on the opposite side from the red gill filaments; they function in retaining food organisms; fishes feeding on very small animals tend to have numerous and long gill rakers.

Gonads: reproductive organs (ovaries of females, testes in males).

Gorgonian: a sessile animal of the Subclass Alcyonaria, Class Anthozoa, Phylum Coelenterata; includes sea fans and sea whips.

Head length: the straight-line measurement from the front of the upper lip to the membranous posterior end of the operculum.

Herbivore: a plant-feeding animal.

Ilicium: the fishing pole and lure of lophiiform fishes, such as frogfishes and anglerfishes, which is used to attract prey close to the mouth.

Imbricate: overlapping; typical arrangement of most fish scales.

Incisiform: chisel-like; used to describe teeth which are flattened and truncate with sharp edges like the front teeth of some mammals, including man.

Interorbital space: the region on the top of the head between the eyes; the usual measurement taken of this space is the least width.

Invertebrate: an animal lacking a vertebral column; includes the vast majority of animals on earth such as corals, worms, starfishes, and insects.

Isthmus: the narrow ventral throat region of a fish.

Keel: a lateral strengthening ridge posteriorly on the caudal peduncle or base of the caudal fin; typically found on swift-swimming fishes with a narrow caudal peduncle.

Lateral: referring to the side or directed toward the side; the opposite of medial.

Lateral-line: a sensory organ of fishes which consists of a canal along the side of the body communicating via pores through scales (when present) to the exterior; functions in perceiving vibrations from a distance.

Lateral-line scales: the pore-bearing scales of the lateral line. The count of these scales (generally from the upper end of the gill opening to the base of the caudal fin) is an important character in the identification of fishes.

Leptocephalus: the elongate, highly compressed, transparent larval stage of some primitive teleost fishes such as the tenpounder, tarpon, bonefish, and eels.

Lower-limb: refers to either the lower edge of the preopercle or the lower part of the gill arch.

Lunate: sickle-shaped; used to describe the shape of a caudal fin which is deeply emarginate with narrow lobes.

Maxilla: a bone of the upper jaw which lies posterior to the premaxilla; in the higher fishes, the maxilla is excluded from the cleft of the mouth, and only the premaxilla bears the teeth.

Medial: toward the middle or median plane of the body; the opposite of lateral.

Median fins: those fins lying in the median (middle) plane of a fish, hence the dorsal, anal, and caudal fins.

Molariform: shaped like a molar tooth, hence low and broad with a slightly rounded biting surface.

Mollusk: an animal of the Phylum Mollusca; unsegmented with a muscular "foot"; often protected by one or two shells; includes snails, clams, octopuses, and chitons.

Nape: the dorsal region of the head posterior to the occiput.

Neritic: refers to that part of the ocean over the continental (or insular) shelf (generally taken from the low-tide mark to a depth of 200 meters).

Occiput: the dorsoposterior part of the cranium.

Ocellus: an eye-like color marking with a ring of one color surrounding a spot of another.

Omnivore: an animal which feeds on both plant and animal material.

Opercle: the most posterior and generally the largest of the external bones comprising the operculum (gill cover).

Operculum: gill cover; comprised of four external bones, the opercle, preopercle, subopercle, and interopercle.

Orbital: referring to the orbit or eye.

Order: a major unit in the classification of organisms; an assemblage of related families. The ordinal word ending in the Animal Kingdom is "iformes".

Origin: the beginning; often used for the anterior end of the dorsal or anal fin at the base; also used in zoology to denote the more fixed attachment of a muscle (the other end being the insertion).

Osteological: in reference to a study of the bony skeletal parts of an animal.

Oviparous: producing eggs that hatch after leaving the body of the mother; this is the mode of reproduction in the great majority of bony fishes.

Ovoviviparous: producing eggs which hatch within the body of the mother and continue development there; the most common mode of reproduction of sharks and rays.

Paired fins: a collective term for the pectoral and pelvic fins.

Palatine: a paired lateral bone on the roof of the mouth lying between the vomer and the upper jaw.

Pectoral fin: the fin usually found on each side of the body just behind the gill opening; in primitive fishes, such as the tenpounders and sardines, the fin is lower on the body.

Pedicellariae: slender three-jawed structures of sea urchins which serve to keep the body clean and capture small prey (the pedicellariae of some echinoids elicit a powerful toxin).

Pelagic: pertaining to the open sea; oceanic (hence not living inshore or on the bottom).

Pelvic fin: one of a pair of juxtaposed fins ventrally on the body; varies in position from abdominal (not far from the anus) in more primitive fishes to thoracic or jugular in more advanced fishes. Sometimes called ventral fin.

Peritoneum: the membranous lining of the body cavity of an animal; its color in fishes may be of diagnostic importance.

Pharyngeal: in reference to the pharynyx or throat region.

Phytoplankton: the plants of the plankton.

Plankton: collective term for the pelagic animals and plants that live above the bottom and drift passively with currents.

Polychaete: an animal of the Class Polychaeta of Phylum Annelida; a segmented worm with setae (bristles); these worms may move freely in the environment or live permanently in a tube.

Polyp: the sedentary form of coelenterate animals consisting of a tubular body with an external opening (the mouth) rimmed with tentacles; may be solitary or one of a colony. The polyp of a coral is the soft living part above the hard skeletal part.

Postlarva: the late pelagic stage in the larval development of a fish.

Premaxilla: the more anterior bone forming the upper jaw; in the higher fishes it extends backward and bears all of the teeth of the jaw. It is this part of the upper jaw that can be protruded in many fishes.

Preopercle: a boomerang-shaped external bone of the head which forms the posterior and lower part of the cheek region; the most anterior bone of the opercular series comprising the gill cover.

Produced: drawn out to a point; lengthened.

Protrusible: protractile; capable of being projected, as in the upper jaw of many fishes.

Proximal: toward the center of the body; opposite of distal.

Ray: the supporting element of the fins; includes spines and soft rays. Also an animal of a major group of cartilaginous fishes.

Recurve: to curve backwards; often used in reference to the shape of a tooth.

Retrorse: curving backward; often used in reference to a spine; the opposite of antrorse.

Rhomboid: wedge-shaped; often used in reference to the shape of a caudal fin of which the middle rays are longest and the sides of the fin are more-or-less straight.

Rounded: refers to a caudal fin of which the terminal border is smoothly convex.

Scute: an external bony plate or enlarged heavy scale.

Segmented rays: the soft rays of the fins which bear cross striations, at least distally.

Serrate: notched along a free margin like the edge of a saw.

Sessile: permanently attached.

Seta: a bristle or bristle-like structure; the plural is setae.

Simple: not branched (in reference to soft rays of fins).

Snout: the region of the head in front of the eye; the snout length is measured from the front of the upper lip to the front edge of the eye.

Soft ray: a segmented fin ray composed of two closely joined lateral parts; nearly always flexible and often branched.

Species: the fundamental unit in the classification of animals and plants consisting of a population of individuals which freely interbreed. The word species is both singular and plural.

Spine: unsegmented bony process consisting of a single element which is usually rigid and sharp-pointed; those spines that support fins are not branched.

Spiracle: an opening between the eye and first gill slit of sharks and rays which leads to the pharyngeal cavity; in rays it serves as the intake for respiratory water.

Standard length: the straight-line length of fish from the front of the upper lip to the base of the caudal fin (posterior end of the vertebral column). This is the length most often used in documenting measurements of various anatomical parts of a fish by ratios.

Stripe: an elongate, horizontal, straight-sided, color marking.

Subopercle: an elongate external bone which is one of four comprising the operculum; lies below the opercle and forms the ventroposterior margin of the gill cover.

Suborbital: referring to the region below the eye.

Suborbital stay: a bony ridge across the cheek of scorpaeniform fishes.

Supraorbital: referring to the region above the eye.

Swimbladder: the hydrostatic organ of fishes; consists of a tough-walled sac just beneath the vertebral column; also known as the gas bladder.

Symbiosis: the living together by two dissimilar organisms. The term includes commensalism whereby one organism derives benefit from the association but the other does not (although not harmed), parasitism where the association is disadvantageous to one of the organisms; and mutualism where both organisms benefit.

Synonym: an invalid scientific name of an organism due to its being proposed at a later date than the accepted name.

Tail: that part of the body of a fish posterior to the anus.

Teleost: refers to the Teleostei, the highest superorder of rayfin bony fishes. The Teleostei represents about 96% of extant fishes.

Thoracic: refers to the thorax or chest region.

Total length: the maximum straight-line measurement of a fish.

Transverse scales: vertical series of scales at the greatest depth of the body (often counted obliquely).

Truncate: square-ended; often used to describe the shape of a caudal fin that has a vertically-straight posterior margin.

Tunicate: a marine animal of the Subphylum Tunicata, Phylum Chordata. Includes the ascidians (commonly called sea squirts), which are bottom-dwelling, either solitary or colonial, and the pelagic larvaceans and salps.

Uniserial: occurring in a single row.

Upper limb: refers either to the vertical free posterior margin of the preopercle or the upper part of the gill arch.

Ventral: toward the lower part of the body; the opposite of dorsal.

Villiform: like the villi of the intestine, hence exhibiting numerous small slender projections. Often used to describe bands of small, slender, close-set teeth.

Viviparous: producing living young which develop from nourishment within and provided by the mother.

Zooplankton: the animals of the plankton.